Discover Northumberland

30 coastal and inland walks

Mark Lejk

Published by Sigma Leisure – an imprint of
Sigma Press, Stobart House, Pontyclerc, Penybanc Road, Ammanford, Carmarthenshire SA18 3HP.

British Library Cataloguing in Publication Data
A CIP record for this book is available from the British Library.

ISBN: 978-1-85058-962-4

Typesetting and Design by: Sigma Press, Ammanford.

Cover photograph: Dunstanburgh Castle © Mark Lejk

Photographs: © Mark Lejk

Maps: Rebecca Terry

Printed by: TJ International, Padstow, Cornwall

Disclaimer: the information in this book is given in good faith and is believed to be correct at the time of publication. No responsibility is accepted by either the author or publisher for errors or omissions, or for any loss or injury however caused. Only you can judge your own fitness, competence and experience. Do not rely solely on sketch maps for nagivation: we strongly recommend the use of appropriate Ordnance Survey (or equivalent) maps.

Foreword

I came to walking quite late in life and now, at 60 years of age, it is one of my favourite pastimes. There is nothing I like better than going out for the day with friends or on my own and preferably rounding it off with a pint of real ale. I am an avid reader of walking books and over the years have tried out many of the better-known walks in Northumberland and the North-East in general. More recently I started to create my own walks, either by adding variations to existing ones, or by poring over Ordnance Survey maps looking for likely paths which could connect together into manageable circular routes. Some of these turned out to be hopeless cases but many resulted in some real treasures. Walks 15 (Weldon Bridge), 16 (Low Hauxley), 21 (Hartford) and 24 (Seaton Sluice) are just some examples of these and they are seldom, if at all, recorded.

I have always been an admirer of Mark Twain's words of advice: "The secret of success is to make your vocation your vacation". I have never really been able to follow this until now. I like walking, I also like writing, I am semi-retired so have time on my hands, so the logic is inescapable – write a walking book. This is the result and I hope you enjoy doing the walks as much as I have enjoyed researching and writing about them. The book has not been written for the serious, seasoned long-distance hiker, although they might enjoy some of the walks. Rather it has been written for the person who enjoys the outdoors and who likes to get out for the day for fresh air and exercise. It ranges from short walks which can be easily be done in a morning or afternoon, combined with a pub lunch for example, to longer walks, taking up most of the day, some in remote areas. As you will find in the body of the book, many of the walks have short and long variations to suit different circumstances.

The over-arching principle in the writing of these walks has been to be accurate. I have often been the victim of misleading, ambiguous and inaccurate directions and there is nothing more frustrating or annoying. All of the walks were walked and tracked by me in 2012 and are accurate at that date. I have made the directions as detailed as possible but things do change so nothing is really guaranteed. I have also annotated the walks with items of interest related to places you meet along the way. Much of this is to do with history but I have included other subjects which interest me personally such as wildlife, architecture, art, literature, recent events etc.

Acknowlegements

Firstly I would like to recognise the anonymous wonder of the modern world, the World Wide Web. I am reminded of the joke about the incredulous, novice computer user who wrote to the famous search engine provider saying "Dear Mr Google, how come you know so much?". Much of the information on the background to the walks was gleaned from literally hundreds of web-sites. I can remember writing up my final dissertation at university, having to go to the library and hand copy extracts from journals. How things have changed. But, as I discovered, not everything can be found on the Internet. I used several books (listed in the bibliography) and these supplied a wealth of extra information. On some occasions I resorted to tracking down and talking to people who would know about certain events. For example, nowhere could I find where the enigmatic cross standing on Church Hill near Alnmouth had come from. I was very surprised. I eventually found out by contacting Fred Bettess of the Alnmouth Local History Group who gave me his recollections of the event. I then contacted the Reverend Ian Mackarill, vicar of the parish of Alnmouth, who consulted Dick Foreman who was churchwarden at the time of the erection of the cross and it was only after this that the sequence of events was finally pinned down. I would like to thank all three of these people for their help. I would also like to thank Christine Ivory for her help in researching the archaeology of the areas covered by the walks. Thanks are also due to the many people I met out and about and with whom I passed the time of day, who often provided me with interesting anecdotes. Fellow members of the CATWalkers Walking Group provided me with much sound advice and encouragement. And finally, I would like to thank my wife, Maureen, for being a patient and encouraging supporter in this endeavour.

This book is dedicated to my grandson, Charlie, who should be walking by the time it is published.

Mark Lejk
April 2013

Contents

About the author

Mark Lejk was born in Sussex in 1952. He moved to Whitley Bay with his family in 1982 and has lived there ever since. He regards the North-East as his spiritual home. He loves the regional identity evident in this part of the world and the humour and friendliness of the people. He took up walking as an escape from the sometimes pressured world of computing in which he worked as a university lecturer. He soon became enchanted by the beauty and history of the area, and Northumberland in particular. He walks regularly either on his own or as part of a walking group which he helped to found. He is now semi-retired but still spends some time in Botswana as a consultant in higher education. He has written a number of academic textbooks on systems analysis and design, so this book is a departure into new territory. It has been a long-held ambition of his to write a book of walks, and retirement has provided him with the ideal opportunity to do so. He is married to Maureen (a true Geordie), has three grown-up children Emma, Katie and Matthew and a grandson Charlie.

Introduction

Northumberland is the sixth largest county in England in area but has the lowest population density. 20% of the population live in urban areas compared to a 73% average for England overall. There are reportedly five times as many sheep as people in the county! These statistics tell their own story. If you want to escape and unwind, Northumberland is the place to do it. Many people overlook the county as they drive through it on their way to Edinburgh and other parts of Scotland. They do not know what they are missing.

The walks in this book will tell you a bit about the history of Northumberland. Many of them visit Bronze Age and Iron Age sites which abound, especially in the north of the county. Other walks tell something of the massive Roman presence centred around Hadrian's Wall. The birth of Christianity in the North-East is mentioned in the holy sites visited on other walks, for example the Lady's Well at Holystone, Church Hill at Alnmouth and St Aidan's Church at Bamburgh. The Norman Conquest is brought to life in the large number of churches of Norman origin which appear in this book. Some of the developing history of the area is told through the castles passed on the walks. Bamburgh, Dunstanburgh, Warkworth, Mitford, Chillingham and Aydon Castles are all visited in this book and their stories are told. The turbulent and violent history of the Border region between the 14th and 17th centuries, epitomised by the Border Reivers, is chronicled in some of the walks. The Industrial Revolution makes its presence felt with references to the lead and coal mining legacy, and the network of disused railway lines which cross the county. And weaving through all of this are the people who took part in this history: kings and queens, bishops, dukes and duchesses, hermits, authors, artists, engineers, sailors, inventors, lighthouse keepers, thieves, smugglers, soldiers, industrialists, characters, eccentrics and ordinary folk. All of these make an appearance in the places visited in this book.

As for the landscape, Northumberland has a serene beauty. It is not as spectacular as the Lake District or the Scottish Highlands, but for the walker, Northumberland is hard to beat. The Cheviot Hills are a great place to escape and, unlike the Lake District, it is not at all busy – it is quite possible to go out for a day's walking and not meet a soul.

The Cheviots are largely an area of igneous rock, grey hard granite which is interspersed with a darker rock from the lava of extinct volcanoes. The lava rock tends to be covered by grassy slopes whereas the granite is covered with heather. The Cheviot Hills are typically smooth and rounded as a result of the weathering of the volcanic rocks.

Another geological feature of the county is the Great Whin Sill, a tabular layer of dolerite rock which stretches from Teesdale to Berwick and makes dramatic appearances as it thrusts up as rocky outcrops through the ground. Bamburgh, Dunstanburgh and Holy Island Castles are all built on Whin Sill as are parts of Hadrian's Wall.

And then there is the magnificent coastline, the stretch from Berwick to the Coquet Estuary being an Area of Outstanding Natural Beauty. The beaches on this coastline are second to none, and for some the golden sand stretches unbroken for miles. A walk along Beadnell Bay at low tide will serve as a fine example. Along this spectacular coastline are some equally spectacular castles – Dunstanburgh, Bamburgh and Holy Island acting as historic beacons along the way.

Between the coast and the hills are the beautiful rivers with their quiet and picturesque valleys. The Coquet, the Till, the Wansbeck, the Breamish, the Aln, the Allen, the North and South Tyne are all clean waterways, and support a large variety of wildlife both in the water and along their banks. To the south of the county is the North Pennines, another Area of Outstanding Natural Beauty, with its bleak moorland and lead mining history. In the west is the Kielder Water and Forest Park, a huge remote man-made enterprise with its own peaceful beauty.

Many of the areas mentioned are protected as they are part of Northumberland National Park, which stretches from near Yeavering Bell in the north down to Hadrian's Wall in the south. It includes the Cheviot Hills, the Otterburn Military Ranges, many of the Northumberland valleys, the Simonside Hills and a large length of Hadrian's Wall.

For nature lovers, over 300 species of birds can be found in the county. On the Farne Islands there are large populations of nesting seabirds such as puffins, guillemots, fulmars, razorbills, kittiwakes, cormorants, shags and eider ducks. On the streams, rivers and reservoirs can be found kingfishers, herons, coots, goosanders, tufted ducks, pochards and many others. The moorland is home to meadow pipits, skylarks, curlew and lapwing. And last of all, Northumberland is home to at least one pair of nesting ospreys in Kielder Forest. As for mammals, foxes, badgers, roe deer, hares, rabbits, otters and wild mink are all present to a lesser or greater extent. The elusive red squirrel can still be found in the area and have been spotted personally by the author on some of the walks (Walks 17, 23 and 30), but have been reported in a number of others. And finally, Northumberland is home to two of its own special groups of animals: the Cheviot wild goats which are descended from domestic goats but roam freely on the hills, and the unique herd of Wild Cattle in Chillingham Park which are visited in Walk 4.

The original broad-leaved forests which once covered much of the county have now all but disappeared, being replaced by commercial plantations of conifers which often dominate the landscape. However tracts of natural woodland can still be found in small patches and many of the walks in this book will pass through them. They are often to be found alongside disused railway lines and there are larger specially conserved areas such as Allen Banks or the fringes of Fontburn Reservoir. In these places you are likely to find oak, hazel, yew, alder, beech, hawthorn, sycamore, ash and other species. Wild flowers abound in spring and summer. These can often be found on the verges of minor roads and lanes but especially in the woods already mentioned.

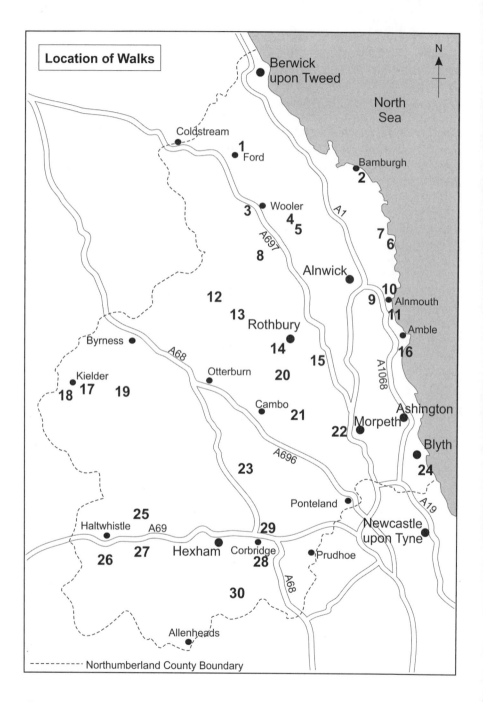

Location of Walks

N

Berwick
upon Tweed

North
Sea

Coldstream

1 Ford

Bamburgh
2

Wooler
3
4
5

A1

7
6

8

A697

Alnwick

10
9 Alnmouth
11

12

13 Rothbury

Amble

14

Byrness

A68

15

16

Kielder

Otterburn

20

A1068

18 **17** **19**

Cambo

21

Ashington

22 Morpeth

Blyth

23

A696

24

Ponteland

A19

25

Haltwhistle A69

29

Newcastle
upon Tyne

26 **27** Hexham Corbridge
28

Prudhoe

A68

30

Allenheads

- - - - - - - Northumberland County Boundary

The Walks

All 30 walks in this book have been personally walked by the author, most of them several times. Many of them have a number of variations where the full walk can be shortened to suit one's needs. Four pairs of walks are in a figure of eight which can be done separately or in one go. Walks 6 and 7 (Craster), Walks 9 and 10 (Lesbury), Walks 17 and 18 (Kielder) and Walks 28 and 29 (Corbridge) all follow this figure of eight format and would make ideal destinations for an extended break. Walkers tend to prefer walks of a certain distance and the walks have been designed to take this into account so that a full range of lengths is available. The walks vary in length from 4.5km (2.8 miles) for the short walk at Allen Banks to 17.8km (11.1 miles) for the walk from Low Hauxley. The variations and combinations of the 30 walks actually make a total of 48 different routes. Below is a table showing these 48 walks in order of distance:

Walk	Place	km	miles
27	Allen Banks short version	4.5	2.8
10	Lesbury – East	4.7	2.9
17	Kielder Duke & Duchess Trail	4.8	3
8	Ingram Valley short version	5	3.1
20	Fontburn short version	5.2	3.2
2	Bamburgh short version	6.1	3.8
9	Lesbury – West short version	6.6	4.1
6	Craster – South	6.8	4.2
7	Craster – North	7.8	4.8
13	Holystone short version	7.8	4.8
15	Weldon Bridge short version	7.7	4.8
28	Corbridge – South	8.1	5
20	Fontburn medium version	8.3	5.2
29	Corbridge – North	8.8	5.5
24	Seaton Sluice short version	9.2	5.7
18	Kielder – Observatory	9.3	5.8

13	Holystone full version	9.5	5.9
27	Allen Banks medium version	9.6	6
9	Lesbury – West full version	10.2	6.3
21	Hartburn short version	10.4	6.5
4	Chillingham	11.3	7
22	Mitford	11.4	7.1
25	Hadrian's Wall	12.2	7.6
14	Simonside	12.7	7.9
3	Wooler Common	12.9	8
11	Warkworth to Alnmouth	12.8	8
19	Black Middens short version	12.9	8
20	Fontburn full version	12.8	8
26	Lambley Viaduct	12.8	8
27	Allen Banks full version	12.9	8
1	Ford short version	13	8.1
2	Bamburgh full version	13.1	8.1
5	Blawearie short version	13.1	8.1
17 & 18	Kielder combined version	14.1	8.8
15	Weldon Bridge full version	14.3	8.9
6&7	Craster combined version	14.6	9.1
5	Blawearie full version	14.8	9.2
8	Ingram Valley full version	14.8	9.2
9&10	Lesbury – combined version	14.9	9.3
1	Ford full version	15.2	9.4
24	Seaton Sluice full version	15.4	9.6
30	Blanchland	15.5	9.6
19	Black Middens full version	14.6	9.7
12	Clennell Street	16.6	10.3
23	Colt Crag	16.8	10.4
28 & 29	Corbridge combined version	16.9	10.5
21	Hartburn full version	17.6	10.9
16	Low Hauxley	17.8	11.1

As can be seen from the list, the walks cover the whole of Northumberland. They are numbered in a basic north/south direction, Walk 1 at Ford being the most northerly and Walk 30 at Blanchland the most southerly.

It has been assumed that walkers will get to the start of the walks by car or bicycle and for many of the walks, this is the only form of transport which can be used. There are of course train and bus services in Northumberland but, as these change from time to time, details have not been supplied. It has been left to the readers to investigate these for themselves.

There are five grades of difficulty for the walks:

Easy
Easy/Moderate
Moderate
Moderate/Strenuous
Strenuous

These grades do not follow any formal system but simply reflect the views of the author, a reasonably fit 60 year old man, after doing the walks. Where walks are considered inadvisable under certain conditions, this is clearly stated in the walks themselves. Particular care should be taken on the three strenuous walks (Walks 8, 12 and 14) and they should not be attempted in bad weather or by an inexperienced walker.

The duration of a walk is notoriously difficult to estimate as we all have different levels of fitness, and walk at different paces. Some people like to stop frequently to take in the scenery or visit an interesting site. In addition, hills take longer than flatter terrain and people get tired towards the end of long walks and slow down. A safe estimate of speed for the walks in this book would be a range of 2 to 3 miles per hour (3.2 to 4.8km per hour) with the lower end of the range being used for hilly terrain and the upper end for flat and easy ground. Add on to this time to visit places of interest and that should provide a reasonable time to work with.

Most, but not all, of the walks have geocaches hidden on them. For readers who are not familiar with this practice, geocaching is an outdoor treasure hunt where players try to find hidden containers containing little trinkets and then report their discoveries on-line. It is great fun and is a good way of getting children interested in walking as every child likes a treasure hunt. Geocaches can be found all over the world – it truly is an international phenomenon. To find out more and register, visit www.geocaching.com. Details of geocaches have been omitted from the walk descriptions as this would spoil the fun.

Several of the walks are well known and versions of them appear in many walking books. For example, the walks at Hadrian's Wall, Craster, Blanchland, Allen Banks, Bamburgh, Simonside and the Ingram Valley are popular classics and rightly so. However, many are not so well known and have been devised by the author through exploration and experimentation. For example, the walks at Hartburn, Low Hauxley, Colt Crag Reservoir, Weldon Bridge, Mitford and Seaton Sluice are seldom reported but they are exceptionally beautiful and interesting.

It goes without saying that walkers should be well-prepared for these walks. An OS map, a first aid kit, a mobile phone (although a signal is not always guaranteed) and a compass or GPS are essentials for the harder and more remote walks. Suitable clothing and footwear should be worn as the weather in Northumberland can change quickly and the winters are cold. You should also leave the details of your route with a responsible person before you set out, just in case.

It is a good idea to carry a pair of binoculars and a camera on your rambles as you never know what you might see, be it a deer, a fox, a kingfisher or even an osprey if you are lucky.

On the whole the walks follow recognised paths such as public rights of way or paths where permission has been granted by the landowner. Some walks go over Access Land, areas which have been opened up by the Countryside Rights of Way Act (2000), and some use paths made available as a result of Stewardship Schemes between landowners and Natural England. However, these latter access arrangements have a limited life span, and where these occur, full details are given in the walks themselves. Walkers should be aware that footpaths can change from time to time as a result of legal diversions. It is also worth noting that a few paths shown on the OS maps do not bear much resemblance to what is found on the ground and so navigational aids may be necessary in such circumstances.

Walkers have a duty to behave responsibly. The Countryside Code which started life as the Country Code in the 1950s was updated in 2012 and is summarised as follows:

Respect other people by:
- considering the local community and other people enjoying the outdoors;
- leaving gates and property as you find them and following paths unless wider access is available.

Protect the natural environment by:
- leaving no trace of your visit and taking your litter home;
- keeping dogs under effective control.

Enjoy the outdoors by:
- planning ahead and being prepared;
- following advice and local signs.

So respect and protect but most of all enjoy.

Walk 1: Ford

Starting from the picturesque model village of Ford, this walk goes through woods and over fields to Ford Moss, then across moorland to the rock art at Goatscrag Hill. It descends to an idyllic hidden waterfall at Roughting Linn and on to the largest decorated rock in England. The walk returns across Ford Moss, through further woods and fields with some spectacular views over Millfield Plain.

You may wish to visit Lady Waterford Hall either at the beginning or end of your walk.The Hall is usually open daily between 11.00 and 16.00 from late March to the end of October but this may change so it is wise to check beforehand. There is an admission charge. Lady Waterford was a talented artist and moved to Ford Castle after she was widowed at the age of 40. She commissioned the Hall to be built in 1860 and it was the village school from then until 1957. She decorated the Hall with paintings of scenes taken from the Old and New Testament, using local children and villagers as the models. The paintings are strikingly beautiful.

Distance	Full walk: 15.2km (9.4 miles) Slightly shorter walk: 13.0km (8.1 miles)
Difficulty	Moderate
Start	Grid Reference NT947375. Ford Village on the B6353 outside Lady Waterford Hall
Parking	There is plenty of free parking in the village
Maps	OS 1:25000 Explorer 339, Kelso, Coldstream and Lower Tweed Valley; OS 1:50000 Landranger Sheet 75, Berwick-upon-Tweed
Refreshments	Ford Post Office serves hot drinks and a selection of cakes. Heatherslaw Mill has a tearoom. The Black Bull in Etal serves lunches and evening meals and has a beer garden
Advice	Some of the fields crossed in this walk have cattle in them

1. With your back to Lady Waterford Hall, turn left up the street past the pleasant village houses. At the top of the street facing Jubilee Cottage, turn right at the junction. You will see the main B6353 road at the top, and you should turn left at the junction. Walk up the road for 150m. There is a lay-by on the right. Turn right through the gate or over the stile along a footpath signposted **Fordhill ¼**. Almost immediately, follow the yellow way mark to the left and head off through the wood, where you will see beech and sycamore among others. Follow another way mark down a short bank with the wood on the left and a fence to your right. You will reach a gate. There are lovely views of the Cheviots to your right and in the summer swallows abound in the fields. At the gate are two yellow way marks. Ignore the one pointing straight on and follow the one pointing half left and walk diagonally down a large field. You will see a row of farm buildings and cottages at the bottom of the field and some trees to the left of these. Head to a gate at the bottom corner of the field just to the left of the trees. Go straight on through the gate. There are likely to be lots of pheasants as the woods round here are used as breeding grounds. Go through

Lady Waterford Hall in Ford

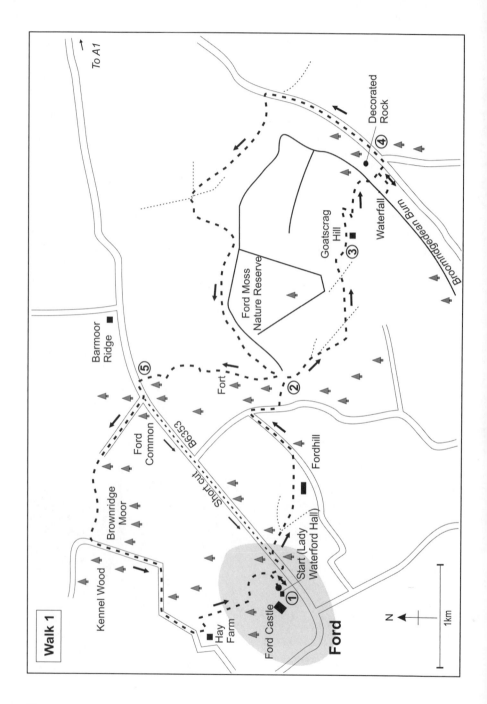

Walk 1

To A1

Barmoor Ridge

Kennel Wood

Brownridge Moor

Ford Common

B6353

Short cut

Fort

⑤

②

Fordhill

Hay Farm

Ford Castle

Start (Lady Waterford Hall)

①

Ford

Ford Moss Nature Reserve

Goatscrag Hill

③

Waterfall

Decorated Rock

④

Brotheridgedean Burn

N

1km

18

another gate skirting the edge of a field. Follow the yellow way mark to the right which goes through a very narrow plantation to meet a track crossing your path. Ignore the footpath marked **Ford Moss ½** straight ahead on the other side of the track as the path is often ploughed over, and turn left along the track. After about 500m the track reaches a metalled road. Turn right here and head for a gate straight ahead across a track leading up to the left of the road. Take the bridleway to the left signposted **Roughtin Linn 1¾** and **Southmoor 2** and follow the track up a hill to Ford Moss.

Ford Moss is a nature reserve managed by the Northumberland Wildlife Trust. It is a peat bog in a large depression and parts of it are actually floating on water. Flora which can be found here include cranberry, cottongrass, sundew and bog myrtle. Wildlife such as adders, cuckoos, roe deer, snipe and the large heath butterfly also make an appearance. This area used to be industrially active. Coal has been mined here since the medieval period, and from the late 17th century Ford Moss was extensively mined with a series of small bell pits and mines into the hillsides. The production of coal was gradually overtaken by the larger and more productive collieries in the north and south of the county where transport links were better. Mining ceased here in about 1919.

Ford Moss

2. At the information panel just before the chimney take the bridleway that sweeps round to the right, skirting the Moss in an anti-clockwise direction. Go through a gate across the path that has a brown **Access Land** sign on it. A little after the gate there is a marker post. Take the footpath signed going slightly right. Later,

as you come out of the trees, the path splits – take the right-hand fork away from the trees (a mixture of Scots pine and oak), rather than the path that carries on skirting the Moss. The path rises on to Broom Ridge. You will see some crags over to the left which is where you are heading. The path climbs to the top and gradually sweeps round to the left. Follow this path all the way taking in the view of the Cheviot itself with its long saddle to your right. You should also be able to catch glimpses of the sea to your left. You may see larks and buzzards on this stretch. You will reach a gate set into a stone wall. After the gate, ignore the path going downhill to your right and go straight on and then bear right. This path is not very distinct and more and more rocks start to appear to your left. You should follow the base of the crags – this is Goatscrag Hill. Roughting Linn Farm will soon be visible down to your right. The path goes through some quite thick fernery and is sometimes difficult to make out. The path goes very close to the crags – in fact you can touch them. You will reach an overhang with quite a wide grassy platform. Spend some time here examining the animal rock art (see below).

The rock art can be found at the eastern end of the grassy platform facing you and are difficult to make out. They are on the flat rock face with a vertical crack bisecting it to the left of the edge of the crags on the platform. They are about 1 metre above the ground and are in the shape of animals – some say deer, some horses – and are carved into the rock. There is considerable debate as to their origin. Some commentators say they are prehistoric, others say they are Romano-British and yet others say they are more recent still. No-one seems to know and that adds to their mystery. The carvings are situated above a rock shelter cemetery where Bronze Age cremation burials were discovered, including two in pottery vessels. Mesolithic flints, indicating even earlier occupation of the site, have also been recorded.

Rock art on Goatscrag Hill

3. You now need to get down to the farm track which you can see leading east away from the farm. If you are brave, you could work your way straight down the hill through the ferns. Or you could carry on round the base of the crags eventually reaching the top and work your way down more gradually. But you need to get to and follow this track which goes straight on, then turns sharp right and over a cattle grid across the Broomridgedean Burn. You should be able to hear but not see a waterfall. Go on for a few metres and just before the track bears slightly to the left take a path to the right going steeply downhill into a gully. Follow this path all the way to Roughting Linn waterfall, going carefully as it is very steep initially and you may have to negotiate some fallen trees. The waterfall is an idyllic hideaway and is a good place to stop for refreshments. You are very likely to be the only one there. Before you get to the waterfall you will see a hole in the rocks on the right. This is a tubular sandstone cave which is large enough at the opening to crawl into but it soon narrows and becomes impassable. It is reputed to be the most northerly cave in England. When you have taken in the delights of the waterfall, retrace your steps back to the main track. Turn right and you will come out on to a crossroads. Turn left, keep your eyes peeled on the wood on your left and you will soon see a very large stone slab through the trees. You will come across a path to this slab. This is the famous Roughting Linn decorative art stone set in a beautiful clearing. In late spring it is surrounded by bluebells and pink rhododendrons. You may want to spend a while examining the fascinating motifs.

This site is famous amongst archaeologists and is a scheduled ancient monument, protected under the law and yet is hidden from view and not guarded by railings or barriers. It is a large outcrop of sandstone and is the largest prehistoric decorated rock in England. The carved motifs are mostly cup and rings but there are other more swirling patterns as well. Close by are the remains of an Iron Age Hillfort, which together with the waterfall and the rock art on Goatscrag Hill, make this small area a beautiful and mystical part of the world.

4. Leave the rock and return to the metalled road. Turn left and follow the road for just over 1km. Turn left through a gate onto a public bridleway signposted **B6353 road 1¼** and **Ford Moss 1½**. Follow the track initially going left then curving round to the right, going

Decorated rock at Roughting Linn

round a mound. The path approaches a barbed-wire fence. Follow
the path along the long fence until you come to a gate about half
way along the fence. This goes into the corner of a field on the
other side of the fence. Go through this gate, turn right veering
slightly away from the fence and head towards another gate visible
at the end of the field. Do not go through this gate but turn left
and follow the path along the field edge, ignoring a gate to your
right leading over a short bridge to another gate, and head towards
Ford Moss. At the right hand corner of the field go through a gate
with a blue public bridleway sign, over a short bridge, through
another gate into the Ford Moss Reserve. Follow the path for nearly
1½km round the Moss just inside the Reserve heading towards the
colliery chimney visible in the distance. Before you reach the
chimney, the path reaches a wood on the right of the track and a
gate crosses the track at this point. Just before this gate is a
footpath marker in a severe state of decay (in August 2011 this
post was lying on the ground and in future may disappear). There
is a fairly obvious footpath to the right and you should turn here
following quite close to a fence and then a stone wall bounding the

wood. When the wall turns left, keep straight on along the distinct path, heading downhill and passing to the left of a small fenced-in pond to a broad track that crosses your path. Turn right on this track past the pond on your right. You will very soon reach a gate – do not go through this but turn left to another gate with a yellow footpath marker pointing straight on (north). Follow the path along the edge of a field until you reach a gate into a wood. Go through the gate and bear right over a little wooden bridge. The path is quite overgrown and will be boggy in wet weather. It comes out onto the B6353.

The woods round here are full of wild flowers. In spring and summer you can find bluebells, forget-me-nots, alkanet, hairy willow herb and Jacob's ladder to name but a few.

5. Turn left on the road and in a few metres you reach a track on the right signed **Restricted Byway**. You have a choice here. If you want to shorten the walk you can carry on for 2km along the B6353 back to Ford. The longer stretch is about 4km and has some fine views looking north. For the longer stretch, turn right along this metalled track and when it turns sharp right to **Watchlaw**, carry straight on to a non-metalled path. Over the top of the rise, the views north to the Millfield Plain and west to the Cheviots are magnificent. Keeping close to the barbed wire fence, you will pass through a gate with a purple Restricted Byway arrow on it and then another gate with a blue bridleway arrow on it. The path will come out on to a minor metalled road. Turn left and follow the road for almost 1½km to Hay Farm and go along the footpath left signed **Ford ¾**. After about 100m, turn left at the junction, go across a small field into a much larger field. Turn right and follow the edge of the field (about 500m), turn left at the bottom and follow this edge of the field. Follow the track through a gate, cross a small bridge and emerge on to a metalled road which takes you back to the Jubilee Cottage in Ford Village.

Ford Castle is an interesting building which started off as a fortified residence in the 14th century, but unfortunately is not open to the public. It once belonged to the Delaval family (see Walk 24) and then passed into the hands of the Marquis of Waterford. It is now used as a Residential Educational Centre by Northumberland County Council. You can see parts

of it from the B6353. A 20 minute walk away from Ford, you will find Heatherslaw Mill which is a working water-driven cornmill on the River Till. A 12 minute walk from Heatherslaw is the pretty village of Etal with its own ruined castle (managed by English Heritage) and the Black Bull which is the only thatched pub in the whole of Northumberland. There is also a light steam railway connecting Heatherslaw and Etal. So all-in-all it is a lovely area not just for a day visit but for longer.

Walk 2: Bamburgh

The centrepiece of this walk is the spectacular Bamburgh Castle which is always in view. Starting from Bamburgh village, the walk heads north and along Budle Bay, then back inland to eventually come out again on to Bamburgh beach. A shorter version of this walk, missing out the return along the beach, passes by the Grace Darling Museum. However the museum can also easily be visited at the end of the full walk.

Distance	Full walk: 13.1km (8.1 miles) Shorter walk: 6.1km (3.8 miles)
Difficulty	Moderate. The walk is pretty flat all the way
Start	Grid Reference NU182351. By the War Memorial on the green at the base of the Castle rock
Parking	If you get there early, you may be able to park on the roadside in Bamburgh for free. Otherwise, there is a car park below the Castle near the start point. In 2012, the fee was £4.40 for all day with lesser charges for shorter stays
Maps	OS 1:25000 Explorer 340, Holy Island & Bamburgh OS 1:50000 Landranger Sheet 75, Berwick-upon-Tweed & surrounding area
Refreshments	There are a number of good tearooms, restaurants, hotels and pubs in Bamburgh
Advice	Try to do this walk when the tide is out to take full advantage of the lovely beach stretches. Some of the fields and tracks get very muddy after wet weather. If you want to visit Bamburgh Castle and the Grace Darling Musuem, you should check the opening times beforehand as they are not open every day all year round

The village of Bamburgh is one of the most visited places in Northumberland and gets very busy at weekends and in the summer months. It is dominated by the spectacular castle rising above the village on a rocky outcrop of the Whin Sill. To the east, the castle overlooks the sea. In the 2007 ITV series *Britain's Favourite View*, Janet Street-Porter chose a view of Bamburgh Castle looking up from the beach. Unfortunately, it did not win the viewers' vote at the end of the series which was awarded to a view of Wastwater in the Lake District chosen by the actress Sally Whittaker who plays Sally Webster in Coronation Street. The general consensus of the people of Northumberland was that there is no accounting for taste!

The castle is owned by the Armstrong family and is open to the public. It is as interesting on the inside as it is magnificent on the outside. The site of the castle has a very long history dating back to King Ida, the first king of Northumbria, in AD547. Like much of Northumberland it had a turbulent history being attacked by Penda, King of Mercia, in the 7th century and sacked by the Vikings in AD993. The Normans built a wooden fortress soon after the Conquest and it was rebuilt in stone in the 12th

Bamburgh Castle

century. The castle was damaged in the Wars of the Roses and was eventually bought in 1704 by Lord Crewe, Bishop of Durham, who also bought the Blanchland Estate at a similar time (see Walk 30). After that time, it served a number of charitable purposes such as providing accommodation for shipwrecked sailors, a boarding school for girls to be trained in domestic service and a free dispensary and surgery. Sir William Armstrong, the Victorian inventor and industrialist, bought and restored the castle in 1894.

1. From the War Memorial, take the surfaced path along the base of the castle rock heading north. When the path bears left in front of a pavilion, go straight ahead on to a stony, sandy path, following it down round the Castle, through the dunes and on to the beach. Turn left towards Harkess Rocks, crossing a stream, and go over the rocks towards a lighthouse. You will pass a white stag painted on a rock after which take the path up past the lighthouse and along the grassy bank just above the rocks. The path meets a beach which you should follow, if you can, round to the magnificent Budle Bay (otherwise, if the tide is well in, go up on to the higher ground). After a while you will round a point and see a derelict concrete pier with some caravans up above it to the left and, just to the left of these, a World War II concrete gun emplacement. Just before the pier turn up the dunes towards the gun emplacement, on the other side of which is a marker post, where you go up the rise along a footpath rather than turning right along a bridleway (the Coast Path). At the top, enter a golf course and go straight on along the boundary past Hole Number 5, then bear right through a kissing-gate to a surfaced lane above a caravan park. When the lane bends to the right, go off to the left through a metal gate along the edge of a field to the cottages at Newtown. At the end of the cottages, go across a track and turn left and then right along the edge of a field boundary. At the top left-hand corner of the field re-enter the golf course through a kissing-gate next to a metal gate and bear half right towards the left of a lookout point at a high point of the golf course. Continue along the grassy path to the left of the lookout heading towards the B1342 road, making sure you look behind you to the wonderful views over Budle Bay. Go through a wooden gate on to the road and turn left along the verge for about 300m to reach a minor road to the right signed **Dukesfield ½**. For the shorter walk, carry straight on back to Bamburgh along the verge of the B1342

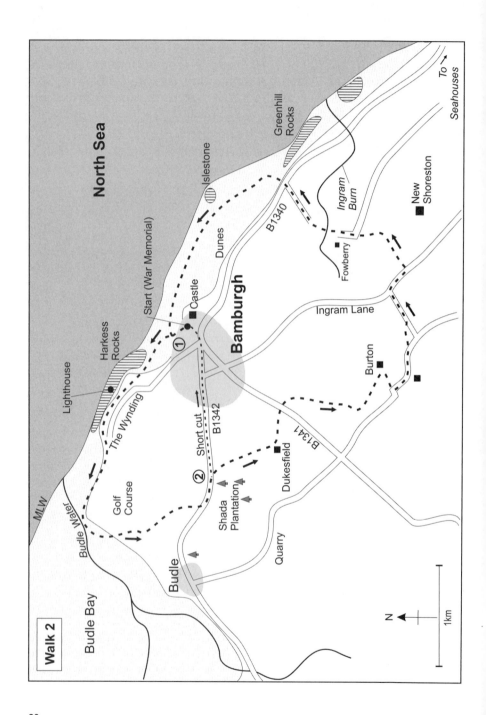

Walk 2

North Sea

Budle Bay

MLW

Lighthouse

Harkess Rocks

The Wynding

Budle Water

Golf Course

Budle

Start (War Memorial)

Castle

Bamburgh

Dunes

Islestone

Greenhill Rocks

B1340

Ingram Burn

Fowberry

New Shoreston

Ingram Lane

Burton

Short cut

B1342

Shada Plantation

Dukesfield

B1341

Quarry

To Seahouses

N

1km

28

taking care as the verge is narrow and the road can be busy. You will pass the newly re-built Grace Darling Museum along the way and St Aidan's Church both of which are well worth a visit.

The RNLI Grace Darling Musuem originally opened in 1938 but was rebuilt and re-opened in 2008 to incorporate the original façade and a new two-storey block. It is a fabulous museum and tells the heroic and sad story of Grace Darling, the daughter of William Darling who was the keeper of the Longstone lighthouse. The lighthouse can be seen from the coast at Bamburgh and was occupied until 1990 when it became fully automated. Grace was born in 1815 and spent her life with four brothers and four sisters in the spartan conditions of a lighthouse family. At around midnight on 6 September 1838, the paddle steamer SS Forfarshire shipwrecked on the rocks near the lighthouse. The next morning, survivors were spotted on the rocks and Grace and her father rowed a four-oared coble in atrocious weather to rescue them.

Grace was only 22 years old and her bravery captured the imagination of the Victorian public. She became a national heroine and celebrity overnight. Grace did not like all of the attention and she sadly died of tuberculosis four years after the rescue in 1842. The original coble boat used in the rescue can be found in the museum. There is an ornate memorial to her in the grounds of St Aidan's Church just over the road from the museum. The church itself was founded by

Grace Darling memorial

St Aidan, the first Bishop of Lindisfarne, in the 7th century. There is a forked beam in the roof above the font at the back of the church and it is said that St Aidan died leaning against this beam outside the church. It has survived two occasions when the church burnt down.

2. For the complete walk, turn right towards Dukesfield and, after nearly 800m, just before a cottage and a house, turn left over a stile into a field, following the side of Dukesfield Manor to the top of a rise and head towards a stile near the top right-hand corner of the

field. Cross a short grassy strip to another stile and then follow the field edge to a stile on to the B1341. Cross the road to a bridleway (often very boggy). Follow the under-used path for almost 900m to pass a cottage and a little further on, turn left over a stile in a field corner (**NB no footpath signs were here in 2012 so be on the lookout for the stile just after the cottage**). Follow the field edge to West Burton Farm where you go through a metal gate past the farm on your left. Walk along the farm lane as it sweeps round to the right towards some white terraced houses. At a junction turn left along the road towards West and East Burton. When you reach a junction with a triangular green, follow the road round to the right. After just over 100m, at a gap in the hedge on your left, go through a gate and bear half right across a field along a footpath. There is foot-path sign here but it is well-hidden by bushes (**New Shoreston 1**). At the other side of the field, cross a stile on to a road and turn left to a junction where you turn right on to Ingram Lane. After about 250m as the road bends slightly to the right, turn left along a bridleway (**Fowberry ½**), pass a World War II bunker and turn left at the bottom of the field along its boundary. You will see the Farne Islands ahead of you. When the bridleway meets a narrow lane, turn left towards Fowberry and just before the entrance turn right up a rutted track. Go through a metal gate and turn left along the field edge to a metal gate, after which you follow a stone wall on your right until you get to a double metal gate. Turn right through the gate towards Greenhill where you go through one of two gates, and follow the lane past the buildings to the B1340. Cross the road, and go on to the beach through the dunes. Turn left and savour one of the finest beach walks in the world back to Bamburgh Castle. Walk all the way past the Castle and turn left through the gap in the dunes which you came through at the start. Head back round the Castle to the starting point.

Bamburgh Beach stretches for 3 miles south of Bamburgh Castle and is so wide and atmospheric that it has been used as a location in several historical films including *Becket* (released in 1964 and starring Richard Burton, Peter O'Toole and John Gielgud) and *Mary Queen of Scots* (released in 1971 and starring Vanessa Redgrave and Glenda Jackson). It is also the scene for the murder of a spy in the more recent film *Elizabeth* (1998) starring Cate Blanchett.

Walk 3: Wooler Common

A walk full of history from Wooler Common over Humbleton Hill and along St Cuthbert's Way. The walk passes between the high peaks of the Cheviot to the south and Yeavering Bell to the north to return along the floor of a quiet valley.

Distance	12.9km (8.0 miles)
Difficulty	Moderate/Strenuous. There is a very steep climb up Humbleton Hill
Start	Grid Reference NT976273. Forest Enterprise car park at Humbleton Burn. To get to the start from the south, head into Wooler (do not bypass it on the A697, actually go into it). Turn left onto a minor road (Ramsey Lane) signposted FE Wooler Common and St Cuthbert's Way – note, this is not the first left, which takes you in a completely different direction. Go along this narrow road for 1.25 miles to reach the car park
Parking	As above. In 2012 parking was free
Maps	OS 1:25000 Explorer OL16, The Cheviot Hills OS 1:50000 Landranger Sheet 75, Berwick-upon-Tweed and surrounding area
Refreshments	Wooler has a good range of places to stay, eat and drink including a youth hostel
Advice	This walk is in the Cheviot Hills so come prepared for changeable weather

The Forestry Commission together with the "Friends of Wooler Common" have made this site a real pleasure to visit. It is used by locals and visitors alike for short walks or as the base for more challenging hikes. There are plenty of information panels around and there is a lovely short trail around two ponds with wheelchair access and a tapping board for the visually

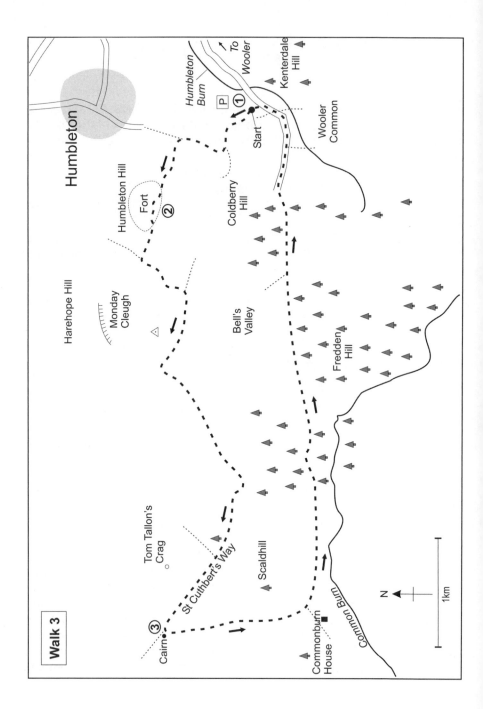

Walk 3

Humbleton

To Wooler

Humbleton Burn

Kenterdale Hill

Wooler Common

Start

① P

Coldberry Hill

② Fort

Humbleton Hill

Harehope Hill

Monday Cleugh

Bell's Valley

Fredden Hill

Tom Tallon's Crag

St Cuthbert's Way

Scaldhill

③ Cairn

Commonburn House

Common Burn

N
1km

impaired. In March you will witness a blaze of yellow daffodils in the nearby Marie Curie Cancer Care "Field of Hope" first planted in 2008. In summer you will be treated to lilac-coloured orchids and the monkeyflower (yellow with blood-red spots) just by the footbridge over the burn at the end of the car park. There are several information boards for trees including Sitka Spruce (named after the town of Sitka in Alaska), Douglas Fir (named after the Scottish explorer David Douglas) and Hybrid Larch (produced by the accidental cross-pollination of the Japanese and European Larch). On the Common on the other side of the road to the car park are the remains of a hillfort called the Kettles. Nearby is the Pin Well where young ladies would wish for love on May Day. The King's Chair is an outcrop of porphyry overlooking the well from where a Scottish king is said to have watched a battle in the distance.

1. From the opposite end of the car park to the entrance, walk over the wooden footbridge across Humbleton Burn. At different times of the year you will find a range of wild flowers here –daffodils in the spring and wild orchids in the summer. A few metres past the bridge is a left turn labelled **dog loop** and then a little further on just past the information panel for the Hybrid Larch is an indistinct sign to the left for **St Cuthbert's Way** which you should take. Follow the path as it rises through the woods to a gate in a stone wall, after which you go across a field still rising to reach a five-bar gate and as a track crosses your path, turn right by an incongruous British Rail parcel wagon. Go through a five-bar gate and descend the clear track where you will soon see Humbleton Hill rising to your left. You will reach a gate on your left at the corner of a field with a clear path to the top of Humbleton Hill (**Hill Fort Trail**). Follow this permissive footpath to the top, stopping frequently to catch your breath as it is steep. You may want to explore the fort and take in the magnificent views.

Humbleton Hill is an Iron Age hillfort, built around 300BC, and is part of a chain of such forts on the edge of the Cheviot Hills. The views of Millfield Plain on a clear day are magnificent and it is easy to see why the site was selected for the fort. Over the centuries its name has changed a number of times – Hameldun, Homeldon, Holmedon and Humbledown all being variations. On 14th September 1402, the Hill was the scene of a famous battle between the English and the Scots, immortalised by Shakespeare in the opening pages of Henry IV Part I. The battle was a victory for the

View north over Millfield Plain

English led by Harry "Hotspur" Percy and the Earl of March and resulted in the death of 800 Scots with only five English dead. Incidentally, Tottenham Hotspur football club gets its name from this very same Harry Hotspur, a member of the Percy family which owned the Tottenham Marshes.

2. Carry on over the hill by descending a path just beside a long pile of stones. Cross a stile at the bottom and a few metres on, turn left uphill on a footpath. Go through a gate and stile on to open moorland going straight on, ignoring any small paths to the right or left, until you reach a post for St Cuthbert's Way crossing your path, where you turn right. After about 700m you reach a fork where you turn left away from a fence and a wall, following the St Cuthbert's Way signs. After another 1km you reach a gate in the wall on your right which you go through and continue along the other side. Almost 500m further on, after passing through another gate and stile, you should veer right off the main track downwards

towards a small plantation still following St Cuthbert's Way. This stretch can get very boggy. Go through a gate on to a stony track along the edge of the plantation and when the trees end, follow St Cuthbert's Way straight on along a grassy path leaving the main track which goes off to the right. Go through a gate in a stone wall next to a ladder stile, passing Tom Tallon's Crag elevated slightly to your right to reach a small cairn. This is where you leave St Cuthbert's Way but you may want to stop a while to take in the views of Yeavering Bell to the north and the Cheviot to the south.

The enigmatically named Tom Tallon's Crag has nothing to do with anyone called Tom Tallon. It is also known as Tom Tallon's Grave or "the auld wife's apronfu' o' stanes"! The name is believed to be derived from the Celtic words *tomen* or *toman* (little hill or mound) and *llan* (enclosure). Yeavering Bell is a massive Iron Age hillfort – the largest in Northumberland with amazing views all around. The fort has two peaks which are surrounded by a wall of rubble. It is believed that the fort contained over 130 timber buildings.

St Cuthbert's Way

3. At the cairn turn sharp left and through a gate next to a ladder stile and follow the path to Commonburn House. When you reach a surfaced road turn left along it away from the farm and follow it for a very pleasant 5km stroll along the valley back to the car park.

St Cuthbert's Way is a 100km walking route between Melrose in Scotland and Holy Island (Lindisfarne). It is normally divided into four separate day walks but there are variations of five and six days. St Cuthbert was a 7th Century bishop and hermit who is regarded as the patron saint of Northern England. In his later years he lived a life of austerity retiring to the Inner Farne Island, living alone in his cell. He was a lover of nature and developed laws protecting local birds including the eider duck which is often known as "cuddy's duck". After his death in AD687 his body was buried at Lindisfarne but nearly 200 years later it was removed by the monks in response to the Viking invasion. The relics underwent a number of journeys but eventually arrived in Durham in AD885. His tomb can now be found in Durham Cathedral. St Cuthbert is one of the most important saints of the Middle Ages and many miracles are attributed to his intercession. The Lindisfarne Gospels are dedicated to him and several churches bear his name. He also gives his name to St Cuthbert's Society, one of the colleges of Durham University.

Walk 4: Chillingham

This walk starts with a visit to the hillfort at Ros Castle and one of the finest views in Northumberland. It then passes through the Chillingham Estate where there is public access until 30 April 2017 courtesy of a Natural England Stewardship scheme. You are very likely to see the unique herd of Wild Cattle. The walk then visits St Peter's Church with its beautiful tomb of Sir Ralph and Elizabeth Grey and continues past Chillingham Castle back to the start.

Distance	11.3km (7.0 miles)
Difficulty	Moderate/Strenuous. There are some steepish ascents at the start of the walk
Start	Grid Reference NU072248. Hepburn Woods Car Park. To get there from the south take the B6346 from Alnwick or the A697 and follow the signs for Chatton and Chillingham until you reach a minor road to the right signed Hepburn and Hepburn Wood Walks. The road and sign come upon you very suddenly. Follow the road through a double bend and at a green gate in the wall on your left, turn right into the car park
Parking	As above. Parking is free
Maps	OS 1:25000 Explorer 340, Holy Island & Bamburgh; OS 1:50000 Landranger Sheet 75, Berwick-upon-Tweed and surrounding area
Refreshments	Chillingham Castle has a tearoom. The Tankerville Arms in Eglingham provides accommodation and is rated very highly. It is not open at lunchtime on Mondays and Tuesdays but is open at lunchtime and evenings for the rest of the week. There is also the Percy Arms at nearby Chatton. Wooler and Alnwick are both fairly close and there are plenty of places to stay, eat and drink there

Advice	The walk through Chillingham Park is along a Natural England Permissive Access Path and access officially ends on 30 April 2017. If you are doing the walk after this date, there will be no public rights of way through the Park, so you will have to contact the Park and go on a guided tour with a warden.
	The walk goes through the Chillingham Wild Cattle Park. These are genuinely wild cattle and are dangerous if approached. You MUST keep to the paths and, on no account, go through the fences separating you from the cattle. Binoculars will come in handy for viewing the Wild Cattle.
	If you want to visit Chillingham Castle, check the opening times in advance. It is not open all year or every day for that matter.
	There are plenty of blackthorn bushes on the last leg of this walk, so autumn is a good time to come if you want to gather the berries for sloe gin.

1. Walk out of the car park and turn right on the road up the rather steep hill. When you come to a National Trust sign for Ros Castle, walk on for 200 metres to a marker post pointing left to a clear path rising up the hill marked as the **red walking trail**. At the top of the hill the view is spectacular, one of the best in Northumberland.

Ros Castle is a 3,000 year old hill fort donated to the National Trust in 1936 as a memorial to Sir Edward Grey who was Foreign Secretary between 1905 and 1916. It was one of his favourite spots. The name comes from either the Gaelic *ros* meaning a promontory or the Welsh *rhos* meaning moorland. At the top is a viewing platform with an interesting topograph and it is said you can see seven Northumberland castles from here. The castles of Lindisfarne (Holy Island), Bamburgh, Dunstanburgh, and Chillingham are clearly seen with Ford, Alnwick and Warkworth reportedly visible on a clear day.

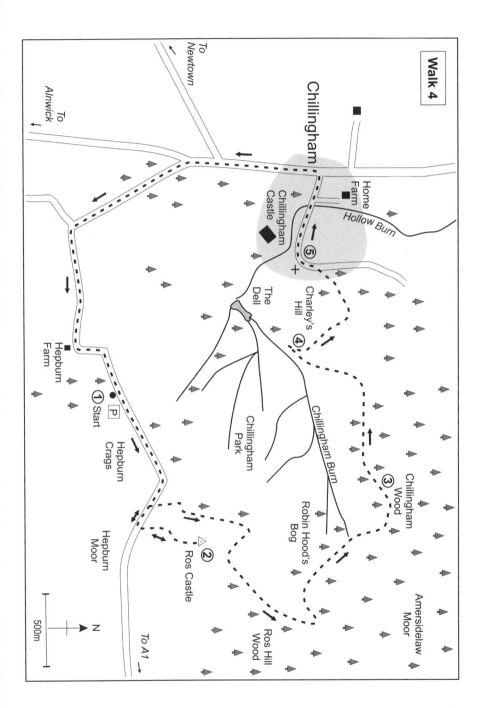

Walk 4

Chillingham

To Newtown

To Alnwick

To

Home Farm

Chillingham Castle

Hollow Burn

⑤

Charley's Hill

The Dell

④

Hepburn Farm

① Start
P
Hepburn Crags

Chillingham Park

Chillingham Burn

Robin Hood's Bog

Chillingham Wood

③

Amersidelaw Moor

Hepburn Moor

△ ②
Ros Castle

Ros Hill Wood

To A1

N

500m

2. When you have taken in the views, return along the path to the road and back to the National Trust sign where you turn right to a gate in the wall. Go through the gate and enter a wood going straight on through the trees along an indistinct path for a short distance to reach a broad track crossing your path. Turn right and follow the green waymarks steeply up the hill. If you look to your left down into the Park, you may be lucky enough to see the Wild Cattle. When you reach a gate with a **Keep Out** sign and a graphic of a bull goring a human (!!), turn right following the green waymark still climbing uphill. When you reach a stone wall, turn left. On the other side of the wall and a little further to the right is Ros Castle, which you have just visited, but there is no quick legal shortcut between the two points. Follow the wall as it enters a wooded area to reach a gate in the wall on your right. Do not go through the gate but turn left and follow the path as it drops down through the woods to reach a broad rutted track signed **The Forest Walk**, where you turn right to reach a wooden gate. Go round the gate, cross a forest road, and go through a high gate signposted **Chillingham** passing through more mixed woodland to another high gate, which you go through to reach a couple of picnic tables with a beautiful view, where you may wish to stop for refreshments.

The woods of mixed conifer and broadleaf trees are teeming with wildlife. Foxes, hares, badgers, red squirrels, roe and fallow deer can all be found here as well as birds such as buzzards, goshawks, green and great spotted woodpeckers, nuthatch, and even crossbills.

3. Carry on along the path going steeply downhill to reach a stony path with open fields in front of you. Turn right along the path and virtually immediately turn left through a kissing-gate leading on to a path between two fields. You may see the Wild Cattle in the field to your left but the Park is big and there is no guarantee. Along the way, go across a gap in the path through a double set of gates which you are advised to cross quickly, and continue on to a junction of paths where you turn left and follow the field boundary. When you reach two wooden gates, go through the one on the right and head towards some buildings, one of which is a ticket office for guided tours of the Park. You will reach a junction of paths near the buildings where you turn right. However, if you have not

managed to see the Cattle, you can go to the ticket office and turn right along a path, across a log footbridge, to the edge of another field where the cattle sometimes congregate. Do not follow this path for long but return to the junction of paths near the ticket office where you now take the path on the left (rather than the path on which you came).

The Chillingham Wild Cattle are unique. It is thought that the herd has been enclosed in Chillingham Park for over 700 years, completely cut off from any other cattle. In fact, because of their isolation, they managed to escape the outbreaks of foot-and-mouth disease in 1967 and 2001 which ravaged the normal cattle population. They are likely to be descended from the earliest wild oxen which once roamed Britain. They are always born white and are believed to be the only genetically pure cattle in the world. They do not sound like normal cattle either. The sound is a sort of hoot or howl accompanied by a low rumbling noise. The cattle are truly wild. When Thomas Bewick was making a drawing for his famous engraving *The Chillingham Bull*, he was chased by the leader of the herd

The Chillingham Wild Cattle

and had to complete his drawing from the top of a tree with the furious animal bellowing and pawing the ground beneath him. The Cattle are now in the care of the Chillingham Wild Cattle Association which has a lease for the grazing rights for 999 years, thus ensuring the survival of the herd. Since 1980, the Cattle Park has been a completely separate entity to Chillingham Castle.

4. Go through a gate in the corner of a field and go straight across moving slightly away from the fence towards the corner of some woods ahead of you. At the top of the field go through a kissing-gate next to a long wooden gate on to a track which you follow downhill, passing a car park on your left. When you reach a sign (**Forest Walk**) to your right, ignore it and carry straight on downhill to a wooden gate. Continue on to reach a crossroads, and turn left to St Peter's Church, which is quite stunning and well worth a visit.

St Peter's Church Chillingham was founded in the 12th Century and is beautifully situated in a sloping graveyard. Inside, in the south Chapel of Our Lady, is a real treasure – the elaborate 15th Century table tomb of Sir Ralph and Elizabeth Grey. The tomb was restored with the aid of English Heritage in 1996. It is very intricate and ornate with a fine sandstone base and the wonderfully detailed alabaster figures of Sir Ralph and Elizabeth lying on top. The tomb is surrounded by niches containing the figures of a host of saints including St Ninian, St Wilfred, St Cuthbert and many more. It really is an unmissable sight.

Tomb of Sir Ralph and Elizabeth Grey

5. After the Church, continue along the road, past an entrance to Chillingham Castle to reach a junction where you turn left. Go along this road for over 1.5km with the boundary wall of the Chillingham Estate on your left, passing the main entrance to the Castle. Blackthorn bushes are numerous on this stretch, so if you come in Autumn, bring a container for sloes. When the road bends sharp right, take the road to the left signed **Hepburn** and **Hepburn Wood Walks**. After almost 1.5km, you will reach the car park.

Chillingham Castle was a 12th Century stronghold which became a fully fortified castle in 1344. It was the ancestral home of the Grey family and then the Earls of Tankerville until the death of the 9th Earl in 1980. It was purchased by Sir Humphry Wakefield who restored and transformed it from an abandoned dilapidated structure into one of the most popular tourist attractions in Northumberland. It is marketed as one of the most haunted places on earth and provides ghost tours and vigils. It truly is a magnificent place with a rich and colourful history and some lovely gardens. It is worth a visit and is especially popular with children who are enthralled by the dungeons, torture chambers and ghost stories.

Walk 5: Blawearie

This walk takes in so much history, it is quite mind blowing. It visits a hidden smuggler's cave on Bewick Moor, a mysterious abandoned shepherd's cottage, a bronze age burial cairn, cup-and-ring marked rocks, an iron-age hill fort, World War II bunkers, and a beautiful Norman church. Take time to do this walk and savour the historical and archaeological wonders met along the way. So, set off early and finish late.

Distance	Full walk: 14.8km (9.2 miles) Slightly shorter walk: 13.1km (8.1 miles)
Difficulty	Moderate/strenuous. Mainly flat but there are one or two steepish ascents and descents
Start	Grid Reference NU101246. If travelling from south of Alnwick, take the A1 north past Alnwick. The road becomes single carriageway after Alnwick for 5 miles. Immediately after the road returns to a dual carriageway, you should take the first left signposted Chillingham, Hepburn, Quarry House and North Charlton. Go straight along this narrow road for almost 8km (5 miles) – you will probably have to open a gate across the road on the way – until you come to a farm next to a very large communications mast. The road dips left here. At the bottom of the dip (after about 100m) the road curves right and there is quite a broad path going to the left across the moor. There is a bridleway sign there for Blawearie. This is the start of the walk so park on the verge near here
Parking	As above, on the verge
Maps	The walk straddles OS 1:25000 Explorer 332, Alnwick & Amble and Explorer 340, Holy Island & Bamburgh; OS 1:50000 Landranger Sheet 75, Berwick-upon-Tweed

Refreshments	This is a remote area. The Percy Arms in Chatton and the Tankerville Arms in Eglingham are the nearest pubs. Wooler and Alnwick are the nearest towns and there are plenty of places to eat and drink there
Advice	Take a good torch if you are planning to visit Cateran Hole. The last section of the full walk can be difficult in wet, windy and misty weather. The shorter walk is recommended in such conditions. Do not rely too heavily on the footpaths marked on the OS maps around Blawearie and on Hepburn Moor. Some of them either no longer exist or are extremely difficult to find. In summer (July and August) there are many insects buzzing around on Bewick Moor. Insect repellant is a good idea.

1. Take the public bridleway across Bewick Moor signposted **Blawearie 2, Old Bewick 3½**. After about 800m you reach a bridleway post and you should turn left off the main track and head towards Cateran Hill. We shall return to this turn-off after visiting Cateran Hole. Cateran Hole is notoriously difficult to find and the best way to find it is as follows. To the left, you will see Quarry House and two masts on either side of it. Ignore the large Eiffel Tower-like mast on the right and concentrate on the slimmer radio aerial to the left of the

Inside Cateran Hole

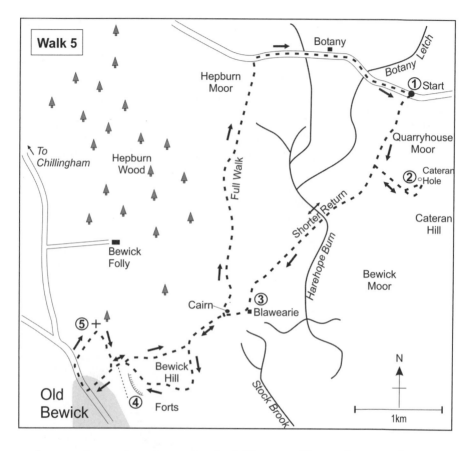

house. As you progress up the hill, you will see this aerial getting closer and closer to the copse of trees near the house. When it just touches the left-hand edge of this copse, you should stop. This should be about 600m from where you turned off the main bridleway. Now head off left across the heather aiming in a straight line directly towards the house. Watch your step as there is no path here. After about 200m you should reach a depression which is largely clear of heather. Cateran Hole is in this depression and the entrance may still be hidden by undergrowth.

Cateran Hole is a mysterious place and has attracted legends over the centuries. It has been adapted by man as there are 6 stone steps leading down to the entrance and the ledge at the start of the cave is shelf-like.

You will need a torch. You may find a sheet of poems written in 2006 and 2007 by a local Northumbrian in a plastic wallet in the cave (it was definitely there in August 2011). You can go quite deep into the cave. After about 35 metres you will have to crawl but soon after, apparently, the cave ends in breakdown. However legend has it that the passage extends for 17km to the Henhole in the Cheviot itself and yet another legend says that it leads to a secret entrance to Chillingham Castle. It would definitely make a good project for an experienced caver! It is generally accepted that it was used by smugglers on the journey to and from Scotland and this is supported by the word *cateran* itself which means "a Highland reiver or freebooter: a robber or brigand generally".

2. When you have finished exploring the cave, make your way back over the heather to the path and then back to the first path on which you started the walk. At the bridleway sign, turn left. Follow this path for about 2km. After a while you will see an oasis of trees ahead of you. This is Blawearie. On the way you will go through a gap in a fence with a gate to the right of the gap. Keep to the main track and as you approach Blawearie you will start to see some ruins. You will go through a dip where the noise of buzzing insects may be very intense as for parts of the year about 20 beehives appear out of nowhere to your right. It is best to go through this bit rather quickly! And then, all of a sudden, you reach Blawearie on a rocky outcrop surrounded by forest trees.

Blawearie is a beautiful, tranquil place built on a rocky outcrop on the moor. It is a ruined cottage, which was inhabited by the Rogersons, a shepherd family, before World War II. It is surrounded by trees (sycamore and plum among others) which were planted in the mid-1800s. There is a terraced garden fashioned out of the rock with lots of nooks and crannies. It seems to be a place where visitors leave hidden stashes of sustenance. If you look in some of the crevices in the rocks you may find well-hidden tins of food. Unopened bottles of wine and beer have even been found buried beneath the leaves!

3. Leave Blawearie along the broad track heading west towards the Cheviot Hills in the distance. At the bridleway marker, go straight on, not half left, and you will see a circle of stones straight ahead of you. Take the little path going half right from the main track towards the circle. This is a bronze age burial cairn. Make your way

Blawearie

onward from the cairn to the main path and carry on. You will reach a stone wall with a gate. Go through this but do not follow the bridleway sign straight on, but go up the track to your left. Keep going straight up the hill ignoring any branches off to the right. The track becomes a small path and as you go over a rise, you should head towards a large rock on your side of a fence. The rock has swirls and rings and cups on it. Behind the rock is a fence, with a wooden beam breaking the barbed wire run to enable you to get across. Cross the fence to reach another large slab with cup and ring marks on it. Make your way along the path by the fence towards the pine trees and you will see some World War II pillboxes and some mounds on your left – an inner and an outer mound – which are the ramparts of an iron-age hill fort. In fact there appear to be two circular forts side by side. You may want to explore this area for a while.

The burial cairn dates from the early Bronze Age and, when first excavated, a jet necklace with over 100 beads was discovered, together with a food vessel. Further excavations in the 1980s gave a clearer picture of this large cairn as a focal point in a larger cemetery, and evidence of cremations included a woman and child in a cist and the remains of two men in an urn. Cup and ring marked rocks (rock art) still baffle archaeologists, but they may represent the earliest evidence of human activity on the moors. It is impossible to give a clear meaning to them as the people lived such very different lives to ours and we cannot see things through their eyes. On the same hill, maybe 3000 years later, the double Iron Age hill forts must have provided good security. There is a steep drop to the west and there are clear views in all directions. And then, thousands of years later, in World War II, more defences were built in the form of two concrete 'pill-boxes' of the 'lozenge' design, constructed in 1940. Layer upon layer of human activity through the ages is represented in this landscape.

4. After exploring the fort, return to the barbed wire fence and follow the path alongside to the pine trees, follow the edge of the trees, and drop very steeply down to the track from Blawearie. Turn left at the track, and go through a gate. Descend towards the settlement of Old

Bronze Age burial cairn

Bewick past an empty old reservoir surrounded by a mixture of trees. Ignore the footpath to the right signposted **Bewick Folly** and come out on to a metalled road where you turn right. After about 400m turn right at a stone cross and follow the road to the Holy Trinity Church.

There is some disagreement about the origins of the name "Bewick". Some say it is derived from the old English *beo-wic* meaning "bee farm", a claim supported by the bee-hives in the area exploiting the abundance of heather. Others say it is derived from *beau* (Norman French for beautiful) and *wick* (Anglo-Saxon for village). The Holy Trinity Church is very old and rather beautiful. The apse (the far end of the church away from the door) dates back to Norman times. The graveyard is worth exploring. There are some interesting memorials and some of the headstones look rather sinister.

Stone cross near Old Bewick

5. With your back to the entrance to the church go straight ahead across the churchyard towards some large horse chestnut trees, cross a stone slab across the Kirk Burn, and follow the wall until you come to a ladder stile. Cross over the stile and turn left along a field edge past some hives, turning right at the corner of the field and follow that field edge uphill to the next corner. Go through the left of two wooden gates at the field corner and return to the main track back to Blawearie. Follow the track for about 1½ km to the burial cairn before Blawearie. You now have a choice. If you are feeling tired or the weather is bad, you can go back to the start via Blawearie by the way you came. It is about 3km of easy going. The longer way is harder but has some fabulous views to the east, west

and north. It is about 4½km. For the longer route, look north from the cairn and you will see a path rising to the top of the hill slightly to your right. Make your way to this path by walking over about 100m of rough ground and then follow the path uphill. When you reach a fork in front of a solitary tree, take the right, broader path. Eventually you reach a metal gate. Go through this and carry straight on. On a clear day, the views are magnificent

Church of the Holy Trinity Old Bewick

and you should be able to see Bamburgh Castle in the distance. Follow the path all the way across Hepburn Moor for about 1½km until you reach a metalled road. You will pass a ruined shieling along the way. The path is sometimes covered in fernery and rather indistinct in places, but if you head due north, you will eventually reach the road. Turn right and follow this road for about 1.8km back to the start, passing a house quaintly named Botany, where you might be able to buy some eggs.

Walk 6: Craster – South

This is the south loop of a figure of eight walk, with Craster in the middle. The north loop is described in Walk 7. They can be done separately or in one go. This south loop heads through woods and across fields to Howick Hall and then towards the sea. It passes Earl Grey's bathing house which is followed by a spectacular stretch along the cliffs back to Craster.

Distance	6.8km (4.2 miles)
Difficulty	Easy/Moderate. Flat nearly all the way
Start	Grid Reference NU257197. Craster Car Park
Parking	There is a parking fee. In 2012 the charge was £2 per day and the ticket also covers the car parks at High and Low Newton on the same day. There is no public parking in Craster Village
Maps	OS 1:25000 Explorer 332, Alnwick & Amble; OS 1:50000 Landranger Sheet 81, Alnwick, Morpeth and surrounding area
Refreshments	The Jolly Fisherman pub in Craster serves food and is famous for its crab sandwiches. The Cottage Inn (just outside Craster) has accommodation and serves food. The Craster Fish Restaurant within Robson's Smokehouse is just opposite the Jolly Fisherman
Advice	If you wish to visit Howick Hall Gardens, they are open from early February to mid-November. Some of this walk goes close to the edge of steep cliffs

1. In the car park, just up from the Tourist Information Office take the signposted footpath (**Craster South Farm, ½**) into the Arnold Memorial Nature Reserve. Carry straight on after the kissing-gate at

the end of the woods, go through a gap in a fence to another gate and go straight up the slight rise. Head towards a row of cottages, through a kissing-gate in a stone wall, and go straight over the road and up a path to the cottages. Turn left past the cottages along a footpath with a stone wall on your left which soon becomes a hedge going through two fields to reach a kissing-gate with a footpath sign to the right to **Howick Hall**. Go through a metal gate at the start of **Hips Heugh** crags and skirt the base until you see a ladder stile and kissing-gate set in a stone wall on your right. Go through the wall across a field to another kissing-gate by the side of a wooden gate. Ignore the bridleway off to the right and cross two fields to reach a track up through some trees to Howick Hall.

Howick Hall was built in 1782 for the Grey family by the architect William Newton of Newcastle. The Hall is not open to the public but the Gardens are and these are fabulous, rated by the BBC's *Gardener's World* as one of the top five coastal gardens in the country. The Gardens are open from early February to mid-November and are well worth a visit. The most famous member of the Grey family is Charles, the 2nd Earl Grey, who was Prime Minister between 1830 and 1834 and architect of the Great Reform Bill of 1832 which led to our modern democracy. Grey's Monument and Grey Street, both in the centre of Newcastle-upon-Tyne, and Grey College of the University of Durham are all dedicated to this courageous politician. Earl Grey tea is also named after him. It was specially blended for him by a Chinese mandarin to suit the water from Howick.

2. When you reach the road, turn left towards the sea, and go straight on for nearly 1km ignoring the left turn to Howick half way along. At a sharp left-hand bend, go straight on through a kissing-gate on to a rutted track. When you get to the sea, turn left along a footpath and head north. You will soon pass an idyllic cottage just by the sea. This is a Grade II listed building and used to be Earl Grey's bathing house. There is no need for detailed directions from here to Craster as you simply follow the path, hugging the coast for nearly 3km, and arrive at the beer garden of the Jolly Fisherman in Craster, where you may like to stop for refreshments. You can finish the walk here if you wish.

Craster is famous for its kippers which are still produced today in Robson's smokehouse, opposite the Jolly Fisherman. There is a shop and restaurant

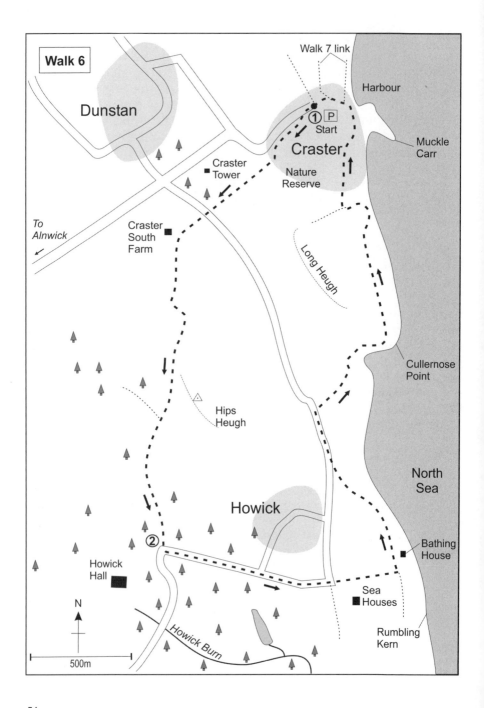

Walk 6

Dunstan

Craster

Walk 7 link

Harbour

① P
Start

Muckle
Carr

Craster
Tower

Nature
Reserve

To
Alnwick

Craster
South
Farm

Long Heugh

Cullernose
Point

Hips
Heugh

North
Sea

Howick

②

Bathing
House

Howick
Hall

Sea
Houses

N

Rumbling
Kern

Howick Burn

500m

54

Earl Grey's bathing house

on site where you can sample and buy the local sea produce. Craster has a small harbour, (partly built from an old whinstone quarry) which was built in 1906 in memory of Captain Craster, killed in the Tibetan expedition of 1904. The Craster family, who own Craster Tower (dated to the 14th century), a short distance to the west of the village, have been associated with the area since the middle of the 12th Century. A medieval village first documented in 1242 lay next to Craster Tower. The present village focused around the harbour dates from the 18th century. Craster also has a small lifeboat station in the harbour which was established in 1969.

Walk 7: Craster – North to Dunstanburgh Castle

This is the north loop of a figure of eight walk, with Craster in the middle. The south loop is described in Walk 6. They can be done separately or in one go. This north loop is probably the most popular coastal walk in Northumberland as it follows the sea to the magnificent Dunstanburgh Castle. The walk returns via the ruins of Craster radar station.

Distance	7.8km (4.8 miles)
Difficulty	Easy/Moderate. Mostly flat
Start	Grid Reference NU257197. Craster Car Park
Parking	There is a parking fee. In 2012 the charge was £2 per day and the ticket also covers the car parks at High and Low Newton on the same day. There is no public parking in Craster Village
Maps	OS 1:25000 Explorer 332, Alnwick & Amble The walk straddles OS 1:50000 Landranger Sheet 81, Alnwick, Morpeth and surrounding area and Sheet 75, Berwick-upon-Tweed and surrounding area
Refreshments	The Jolly Fisherman pub in Craster serves food and is famous for its crab sandwiches. The Cottage Inn (just outside Craster) has accommodation and serves food. The Craster Fish Restaurant within Robson's Smokehouse is just opposite the Jolly Fisherman
Advice	If you plan to visit Dunstanburgh Castle during the winter months, you should check opening times as it is closed for some days during the week (in 2012/13 it was only open on Saturdays and Sundays from 5 November to 28 March)

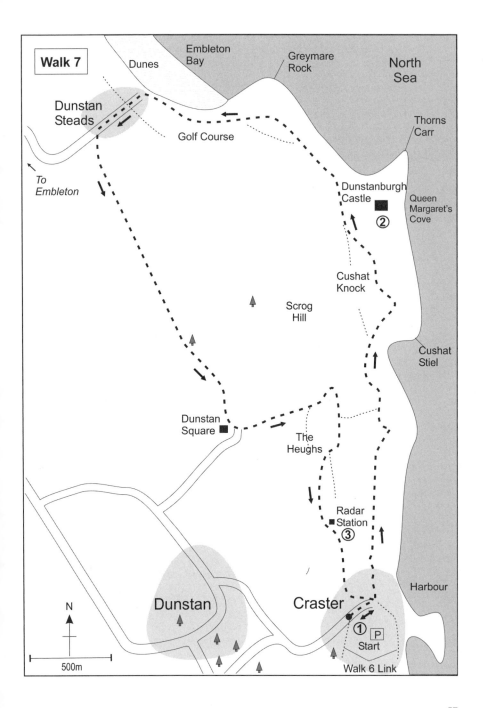

Walk 7

Embleton Bay

Dunes

Greymare Rock

North Sea

Dunstan Steads

Golf Course

Thorns Carr

To Embleton

Dunstanburgh Castle ②

Queen Margaret's Cove

Cushat Knock

Scrog Hill

Cushat Stiel

Dunstan Square

The Heughs

Radar Station ③

Harbour

N

Dunstan

Craster ① P Start

Walk 6 Link

500m

Dunstanburgh Castle

1. If you have just done Walk 6, turn right to the harbour after the Jolly Fisherman, past the smokehouse. If you are starting from Craster car park, head right out of the car park to the harbour. At the harbour, follow the path for nearly 2km along the coast all the way to Dunstanburgh Castle. You may like to visit the Castle.

Dunstanburgh Castle is managed by English Heritage but National Trust members can also visit for free. It is open all year round but not every day of the week during the winter months. It truly is a magnificent sight built on a rocky promontory overlooking the north. It is a ruin but it still must be one of the most photographed and visited sites in Northumberland and you can see why. It is stunning. Although it is by far the largest castle in Northumberland in area, it played little part in its history. The castle was built in 1313 by Thomas, Earl of Lancaster, who was a cousin of King Edward II, but as is the way with royalty, Thomas was one of the King's fiercest opponents. Thomas was responsible for the execution of Piers Gaveston who was Edward II's favourite and built the castle soon afterwards as a means of protection but also to show he was just as important as the king. Thomas was eventually executed for treason but the castle stayed in the House of Lancaster and during the Wars of the Roses it was taken and re-taken five times and much of it was destroyed by artillery. Since Tudor times, it has been a ruin. It is such a dramatic and beautiful place that Turner painted it three times.

Just before reaching the castle, several earthworks have been identified to the south and west of the castle including medieval fish ponds and cultivation systems. Later activity is represented by a six metre wide anti-tank ditch from the World War II which is just north of the medieval earthworks.

2. Facing the Castle, at the wooden gate at the entrance, take the path immediately to the left away from the sea, skirting round the base of the castle. It drops down to meet a public footpath and you will soon see the lovely Embleton Bay straight ahead. Go along the path with Embleton Golf Course on your left past some World War II pillboxes. Take the path to your left which goes across the golf course towards some buildings, going through a gate on to a metalled road to reach the buildings (Dunstan Steads). Turn left at the bridleway (**Dunstan Square 1**) and follow this all the way to the farm at Dunstan Square. At the farm take the footpath left through

a metal gate along the edge of a field (**Craster 1, Dunstanburgh Castle 1¼**). At the bottom of the field go through a wooden gate and head towards the gap in the cliffs ahead. When you arrive at the top you will see Dunstanburgh Castle again and you should go through the gate in the field corner on your right with a green National Trust sign on it. Go diagonally right across the field towards the ridge and walk along the ridge until you meet two empty concrete buildings. This is the Craster radar station.

Craster radar station was a top-secret installation used in World War II. The stretch of coast between Embleton Bay and Craster has been the subject of a detailed exam-ination by the National Trust and English Heritage and the study revealed a set of defences to guard against the possible invasion by the Germans along this stretch of coast. These include anti-tank blocks, pill boxes and the remains of machine

The remains of Craster radar station

gun nests, weapons pits and a minefield. In 1944 the radar station was dismantled and the site was used to house Italian prisoners-of-war who fashioned a terraced garden on the slopes behind the building.

3. Make your way from the radar station along the track towards the village which descends to meet a fence alongside a field. Follow the fence and just before the village, go over a stile, follow the path by a stone wall, and turn sharp left behind a house to meet a road down to the village. Turn right to return to the car park.

Walk 8: Ingram Valley including Linhope Spout

This can be either an easy or a very difficult walk depending on whether the short or long versions are taken. The shorter walk is a popular day out as it visits the picturesque Linhope Spout, the largest waterfall in the Cheviot Hills, and then returns to the start. The full walk is a very different matter and goes up into the wilderness on the moors and then down again to follow the River Breamish back to the start.

Distance	Full walk: 14.8km (9.2 miles) Shorter walk to Linhope Spout and back: 5.0km (3.1 miles)
Difficulty	Full walk: Strenuous; Shorter walk: Easy
Start	Grid Reference NT977162. To get to the start, take the A697 north through Powburn, cross the River Breamish and after about 700m turn left towards Ingram. Follow this narrow road for about 9km to Hartside, where the public road stops and is replaced by a private road
Parking	On the side of the road near Hartside just before a junction where there is a sign indicating a private road
Maps	OS 1:25000 Explorer OL16, the Cheviot Hills; OS 1:50000 Landranger Sheet 81, Alnwick, Morpeth and surrounding area
Refreshments	The nearest place for refreshments is Powburn where there is a service station and a pub (The Plough). The Queens Head in nearby Glanton is also well thought of but check out beforehand whether it is open, as it is sometimes empty due to changes of ownership

Advice	The full walk will be difficult in wet and windy weather and especially when visibility is poor or there is snow on the ground. A map and compass are absolutely essential over the high ground. A walking stick will come in handy especially for the descent from High Cantle to the valley floor

The Ingram Valley is thought by many to be the most beautiful of the Northumberland valleys. It is also the most accessible. The drive to the start along the narrow road from Ingram follows the River Breamish and there are plenty of lovely grassy places to stop for a picnic.

1. From the parking space, follow the road straight on past Hartside (**Linhope 1, Linhope Spout 1½**) through a white metal gate, and after about 1¼km you reach the tiny hamlet of Linhope. Linhope is a pretty little hamlet with some picturesque houses. As you head into Linhope, you may glimpse Linhope Lodge, ahead of you and slightly to the right, hidden in the trees above the other houses. It was built by Lord Joicey of Ford Castle in 1905, in the style of a bungalow from British India. Keep on the road as it bears left, then take the right hand fork through a wooden gate into a field where you immediately turn right. Go along the edge of the field to join a red gravel track rising uphill to a kissing-gate next to a larger gate which you go through on to Access Land and carry straight on rising all the time. Ignore a bridleway sign leading off uphill to the left (which we shall return to later) and go straight on until the trees on your right come to an end. Turn right towards Linhope Spout and follow the path through a kissing-gate. Just after a wooden finger-post to Linhope Spout, the path forks. Both forks lead to the waterfall. The left fork goes to the top of the fall and descends down. The right one is quicker but can get muddy and leads directly on to the banks of Linhope Burn. You will want to spend some time enjoying the waterfall.

Linhope Spout is the largest waterfall in the Cheviot Hills plunging 18 metres into a 5 metre deep plunge pool. After wet weather it is an impressive sight and the noise can be heard as far away as Linhope. In the summer months, you will often find youngsters jumping into the pool

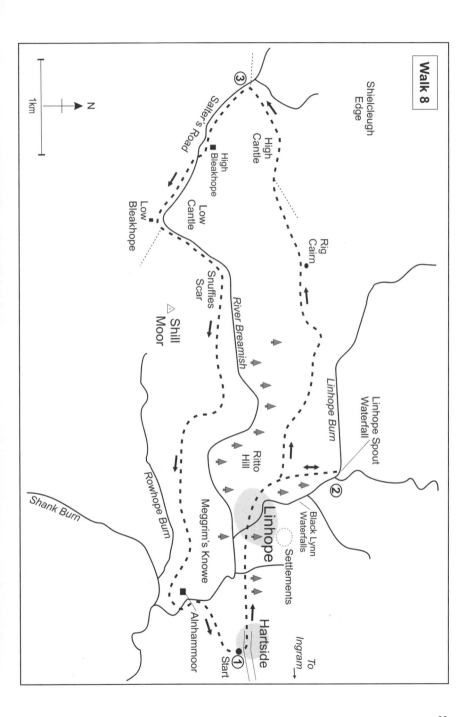

Walk 8

Shielcleugh Edge

Salter's Road

High Cantle

③

High Bleakhope

Low Cantle

Low Bleakhope

Rig Cairn

River Breamish

Snuffies Scar

△ Shill Moor

Linhope Spout Waterfall

Linhope Burn

Ritto Hill

Rowhope Burn

Shank Burn

Meggrim's Knowe

Black Lynn Waterfalls

Linhope

Settlements

②

Alnhammoor

Hartside

Start ①

To Ingram →

N

1km

Linhope Spout

from surrounding rocks – an activity which is not recommended. It is surrounded by pleasant grassy banks, ideal for a picnic.

2. From the waterfall, make your way back to the red gravel path and turn left to reach the marker post with a bridleway sign pointing uphill sharply to your right (almost going back on yourself). If you are doing the shorter walk, re-trace your steps back to the car. For the full walk, follow the path uphill to reach a wooden gate next to a stile which you cross on to a thin path through the grass. Go straight on along this rather indistinct path ignoring any wider paths to the left and right, always going in a westerly direction. Eventually you will see a fence ahead of you crossing your path with a wooden gate slightly to your left and a double stile slightly to your right. The official bridleway crosses the stiles, but it is more straightforward to go through the gate to your left and follow the clear path in a westerly direction. **Be careful on this stretch of nearly 3km to High Cantle as you are really in the wilds and it can be very boggy and wet. The path shown on the Ordnance Survey Explorer map shows very straight segments which are quite misleading. The path on the map goes slightly north of Rig Cairn whereas we go actually right to it. Our route basically follows the map path but slightly to the south of it.** You should ignore any path off to the left and just go straight along the clear path in a westerly and then west-south-westerly direction. You should reach Rig Cairn (pile of stones), the highest point, after about 1.6km and then High Cantle after a further 1.2km where you should go through a gate and a stile straight ahead of you. Follow the bridleway across the heather to another gate and stile which you cross and head towards a marker post straight ahead. Follow the bridleway as it works its way downhill, initially gradually and then very steeply, passing through a gate next to a stile in a wire fence to eventually reach the valley floor.

From April onwards, you are very likely to see curlews on the moors. Just like the kittiwake, its name is believed to be derived from its distinctive cry. It is the largest of the British waders and has a long downward curving bill. It is a common bird in Northumberland and is used as the logo for the Northumberland National Park.

The hills around here are full of ancient remains. For example, on Ritto Hill which is passed on the way to Rig Cairn, there is evidence of a small Bronze

Ingram Valley

Age settlement with two hut circles and two settlements of Roman date are also nearby.

3. At the bottom, turn left and follow the restricted byway through a number of gates for 1.6km to reach the farm of Low Bleakhope, passing High Bleakhope along the way. This track is part of the Salter's Road. It is very clear and follows the River Breamish crossing from the north to the south side after High Bleakhope. At Low Bleakhope, follow the track round to the left, and keep going for a lovely stretch of 4.4km starting close to the river and then rising away from it to reach the farm at Alnhammoor. Keep on the track past Alnhammoor, following it round to the left and crossing a bridge over the River Breamish to eventually reach the junction from where you set off (1.2km after Alnhammoor).

High Bleakhope features in the life of the late Willie Taylor, the Cheviot shepherd, fiddle player and composer who died in 2000 at the age of 84. As a young man Willie worked alongside Geordie Armstrong, another hill shepherd and fiddle player, and they both lodged at High Bleakhope. This period was influential in the development of Willie Taylor's style. In recent years, traditional Northumbrian music has experienced something of a revival and Willie Taylor's tunes are now part of the repertoire of many musicians. He has had a tremendous influence on the younger generation of musicians, in particular Kathryn Tickell who plays the fiddle and the wonderfully mellow Northumbrian Pipes.

Salter's Road is a medieval route believed to have been taken by traders transporting salt from the coast to Scotland. In keeping with the colourful history of the area, it was at first called "The Thieves Road" as it was a dangerous route frequented by bandits.

Walk 9 : Lesbury – West

This is the west loop of a figure of eight walk, with Lesbury in the middle. The east loop is described in walk 10. They can be done separately or in one go. This west loop goes inland along the River Aln and then turns back east along a disused railway track through the land of the Northumberland Estates and returns to Lesbury via Alnmouth Station. It can be shortened at a point along the way.

Distance	Full walk: 10.2km (6.3 miles) Shorter walk: 6.6km (4.1 miles)
Difficulty	Moderate. Flat all the way
Start	Grid Reference NU235117. Lesbury
Parking	On the roadside in Lesbury
Maps	OS 1:25000 Explorer 332, Alnwick and Amble. OS 1:50000 Landranger Sheet 81, Alnwick, Morpeth and surrounding area
Refreshments	The Coach Inn in Lesbury. Also there are several pubs and cafes in nearby Alnmouth. The Red Lion is a particular favourite with a lovely beer garden overlooking the River Aln
Advice	This walk crosses land owned by the Northumberland Estates who have granted the public permission to walk on their land. The longer walk follows a disused railway track which is not a public right of way. If permission is revoked at any time, you will only be able to do the shorter walk which is made up completely of public rights of way. The walk can get muddy in places so come prepared

1. From Lesbury, go back to the A1068. Before you get to the roundabout, turn left on to a tarmacced path and cross the old bridge over the River Aln to the A1068. Cross the road and through

a gate into a field on to a footpath (**Bilton Mill 1½, Alndyke 2¼**). There is an information panel here which describes walks on the Northumberland Estates, parts of which we shall be doing. Follow the path at first uphill and then down towards the river with the railway line on your left. Go along the river to reach Alnmouth Viaduct and continue hugging the river to Bilton Mill. You will see several water birds on this stretch including the goosander with the female having a lovely orange-red head with a shaggy crest. At Bilton Mill, go round the buildings circling them, then keep going along the track by the river, ignoring the path off to the left. After a while the track turns sharp left. There are supposed to be some stepping stones across the river here, but use them at your peril. It looks nigh on impossible to cross with any degree of safety. In any case, we are not crossing the river. If you are doing the shorter walk, turn left and follow the track to a bridge over a disused railway line and then resume at Paragraph 3. For the longer walk, continue to the next paragraph.

Goosanders on the River Aln

The old bridge over the River Aln is also known as Lesbury Mill Bridge. It was built in the 15th Century and is Grade I listed. It may have been built at the same time as Lesbury Mill which stood next to the bridge. Until recently, this was the road bridge carrying the A1068 over the river, but was replaced in 2004 by the new bridge with the tubular spans. The railway viaduct over the River Aln was built in 1848-9 by Robert Stephenson and is part of the East Coast main line.

2. Go straight on off the track and head down to a footbridge over Cawledge Burn and keep following the river for about 800m until the river bends away to the right. At this point, go straight on to a

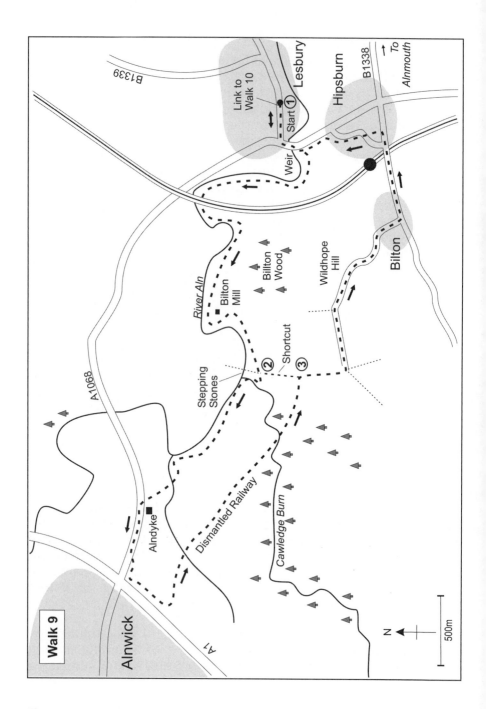

Walk 9

Alnwick

B1339

Lesbury

Link to
Walk 10

Start ①

Weir

Hipsburn

B1338

To
Alnmouth

Bilton

Bilton Wood

Wildhope Hill

River Aln

Bilton Mill

Shortcut

②

③

A1068

Stepping Stones

Alndyke

Dismantled Railway

Cawledge Burn

A1

N

500m

70

metal gate. Just before the gate, follow the yellow waymark left along the field edge to reach a gate on your right which will take you down to a footbridge over Willow Burn. Climb a hill to a metal gate with a stile by its side. After the gate go half left across a field towards the busy A1068. Go through a white metal gate and turn left along the road. Just after the sign showing you are entering the town of Alnwick, you will see an information panel showing the walk you are on. Turn off the road here and follow the yellow dotted path shown on the panel alongside the A1068 towards the A1. When you reach a barn, pass to the right of it, to reach a fenced-in path (often very muddy) to the left following very close to the A1. After about 300m going uphill, the path bears left on to a dismantled railway line. Follow this very pleasant and quiet track for almost 2km to reach a bridge over the track. Don't go under the bridge but head up to the right just before it to reach the track over the bridge. This is where we rejoin the shorter walk.

This walk passes through the Northumberland Estates which represents the business interests of the Duke of Northumberland, a member of the Percy family. The Estates have a number of other trails open to the public in or near Alnwick. The Percy family have owned Alnwick Castle since 1309 and the castle is the setting for Hogwarts School in the Harry Potter films. It is still used as the family home of the Duke and his family. The Estates has a large property portfolio including retail and business parks. It also owns a number of historic buildings including Warkworth Castle and Prudhoe Castle in Northumberland and Syon House in London.

3. If you are doing the shorter walk, carry straight on over the bridge. If you are doing the longer walk, turn right after climbing up to the bridge. Follow the cycleway to reach a house called the Huntsman's House and turn left on to a very minor road ignoring the footpath straight on to **Spy Law**. Follow the road as it bends sharp right, then on to Bilton House and then Bilton. When you reach a road junction at Bilton, turn left towards Alnmouth Station, signed **Alnmouth 1½**. Go over the railway bridge past Alnmouth Station. After the bridge turn left down Curly Lane through a housing estate to reach the A1068 where you turn left and back to Lesbury.

Lesbury has one of the most interesting place names in Northumberland as it is derived from the Old English *Laeces Byrig*, the dwelling of the leech

or physician. No-one really knows where the name came from but it is easy to see how it has evolved over time into Lesbury. St Mary's Church in Lesbury was founded in the 12th Century on the site of a Saxon building. A brief description of the Church and a couple of its colourful vicars can be found in Walk 10 which continues the figure of eight to Alnmouth and back.

Walk 10: Lesbury – East to Alnmouth

This is the east loop of a figure of eight walk, with Lesbury in the middle. The west loop is described in Walk 9. They can be done separately or in one go. This east loop is one of the loveliest short walks in Northumberland approaching Alnmouth along the River Aln and going past the iconic coloured terraces. It returns through meadows along the river where water birds can be viewed in abundance.

Distance	4.7km (2.9 miles)
Difficulty	Easy. A lovely short walk, mostly flat apart from a short rise and descent on leaving Alnmouth
Start	Grid Reference NU235117. Lesbury
Parking	On the roadside in Lesbury
Maps	OS 1:25000 Explorer 332, Alnwick and Amble. OS 1:50000 Landranger Sheet 81, Alnwick, Morpeth and surrounding area.
Refreshments	The Coach Inn in Lesbury. Also there are several pubs and cafes in nearby Alnmouth. The Red Lion is a particular favourite with a lovely beer garden overlooking the River Aln
Advice	This is the shortest walk in the book but is absolutely beautiful. It has a romantic feel about it and can be done in a couple of hours if that. Combined with a pub lunch in Alnmouth, it makes for a great day out

1. From the Coach Inn in Lesbury, carry on down the street on the right hand side away from the A1068, pass the Church of St Mary and as the road bends left, carry straight on to the right of a couple of houses (numbered 1 and 2) on to a footpath (**Alnmouth Road ½**). Cross a footbridge over the River Aln (footpath sign **Hipsburn ¼**). Just after an electricity sub-station take a footpath off to the left (**Alnmouth Road ¼**), ignore the Natural England permissive access

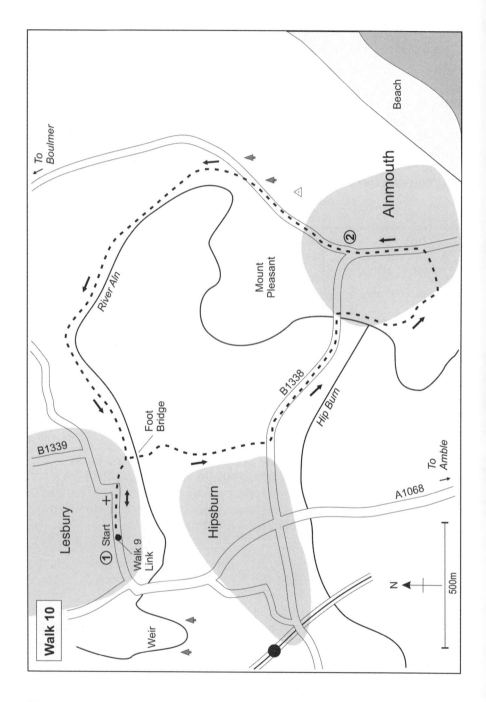

Walk 10

Beach

Alnmouth

To Boulmer

River Aln

Mount Pleasant

②

Foot Bridge

B1338

Hip Burn

B1339

Lesbury

① Start

Walk 9 Link

Hipsburn

To Amble

A1068

Weir

N

500m

path to the left, and follow the path along the edge of a football field to the B1338 road into Alnmouth. Turn left along the road to reach a bridge. On the other side of the bridge, cross right over the road and take the footpath signed **Lovers Walk and Coast Walk**. Go down some steps and follow the wonderful path along the river, taking in the cross on Church Hill over the river and the iconic coloured terraced houses which people can see from the train on their way to Scotland. Pass a children's playground on your right to reach a narrow lane which you cross and go straight ahead on to Garden Terrace. Turn left up the main street of Alnmouth, where you may want to stop at one of the pubs.

The Church of St Mary in Lesbury is Norman in origin and was restored by Salvin in 1846. It has a medieval font and some lovely stained glass windows. Two of the vicars of Lesbury are worthy of mention. Percival Stockdale (1736 – 1811) was at one time a friend and neighbour of Samuel Johnson. He was a poet and author who enjoyed some reputation in his day. He was rather eccentric and is thought to have been the model for a

The coloured terraces at Alnmouth

character called Belfield in Frances Burney's popular 18th century novel *Cecilia*. Incidentally, in the last few pages of this novel, a Dr Lyster uses the words "Pride and Prejudice" a number of times and it is thought that this is where Jane Austen got the idea for the title for her masterpiece. Another vicar of note is Patrick Mackilwyan, who lived to the age of 101. He had a reputation for being very quarrelsome but won the respect of his parishioners during the Plague of 1665 when, at the age of 97, he attended to the sick who had been removed into tents on the nearby moor.

2. The street reaches a roundabout where you go straight on along the road to Boulmer following it uphill past an old school which is now an art gallery (which you may want to visit). Ignore any footpaths off to your right and after you pass a couple of wooden benches take the footpath downhill to your left (**Lesbury 1**). Cross a ladder stile and head down towards the river, go through a gate

Alnmouth

or over the ladder stile next to it, and past a wooden bench to reach the river. Turn right and follow the path close to the river. You will find an abundance of water birds here. Follow close to the river through some gates and over stiles and when the wooden fence on your right goes uphill, follow alongside away from the river. Follow the path to a field and continue with the river close to your left for just over 500m. Cross a wooden footbridge over a burn to reach the footbridge you crossed at the start of the walk where you turn right back to the start.

Alnmouth is a picturesque little village, famous for the view of the coloured terraced houses from the passing trains on the East Coast line. It was set up as a seaport in about 1150 and its fortunes went up and down over the centuries. The 18th and early 19th Century was its most prosperous period, the principal export being corn. Timber was imported from Norway and goods from London, Holland and elsewhere. It had a reputation for smuggling and prompted John Wesley in 1748 to describe it as "a small sea-port town famous for all kinds of wickedness"! The coastal trade gradually dwindled away with competition from the railways and the inability of the harbour to cope with larger iron and steel ships. The town survived however as it became a popular tourist destination with some wealthy families building holiday homes. It remains a popular place to visit to this day.

Walk 11: Warkworth to Alnmouth

This walk follows the coast northwards from Warkworth to just south of Alnmouth where it visits the historic Church Hill and its iconic cross with beautiful views over the mouth of the River Aln. It returns across fields and then follows the north side of the River Coquet from which Warkworth Castle can be seen in all its glory. This last stretch is open to the public until May 2020 as part of a Natural England Stewardship Scheme, and an alternative route is included for walks after this date.

Distance	12.8km (8.0 miles)
Difficulty	Moderate. Flat nearly all the way
Start	Grid Reference NU254064. Warkworth Dunes Picnic Site. Go north through Warkworth on the A1068. Immediately after the bridge over the River Coquet turn right on to a narrow road signposted for the Cemetery, Beach and Warkworth Golf Club. Follow the road straight on for just over 500m. You will reach a sharp left turn and the picnic site is just after this on the right
Parking	As above. In 2012, parking was free
Maps	OS 1:25000 Explorer 332, Alnwick & Amble OS 1:50000 Landranger Sheet 81, Alnwick, Morpeth and surrounding area
Refreshments	There are plenty of places to eat and drink in Warkworth
Advice	This walk can be done at any time but is perhaps best when the tide is out to take full advantage of the beach section at the start

1. From the car park, take the public bridleway towards the beach. When you get to the dunes, ignore the footpath to the left and go straight on to the beach. You will see Coquet Island to your right.

Turn left up the beach and head north for almost 1km. As you approach the rocks of Birling Carrs turn left at a gap in the dunes by a red lifebelt and head up the gully beneath a wooden bridge across the golf course. Go up a short rise, through an opening in a fence and turn right on to a track. Follow the track round across the golf course and through a caravan park. Drop down from the caravan park, cross a wooden footbridge and enter the National Trust Alnmouth Dunes site. Follow the broad track straight on alongside a stone wall to your left. At the end of the dunes, go past a metal gate and carry straight on past a large ruined barn (this is actually a Grade II listed building as it is thought to be the only example in the country of a guano shed). When the track turns sharp left, go with it, ignoring the path straight on. After a few metres turn right past a metal gate and follow the bridleway towards Church Hill where you should see a wooden cross at the top. Follow the path as it skirts round the marsh to reach Church Hill, which you may wish to explore a little. On the Ordnance Survey map this area is shown as covered in water but it is really a relatively dry marsh most of the time.

St Cuthbert's Cross on Church Hill

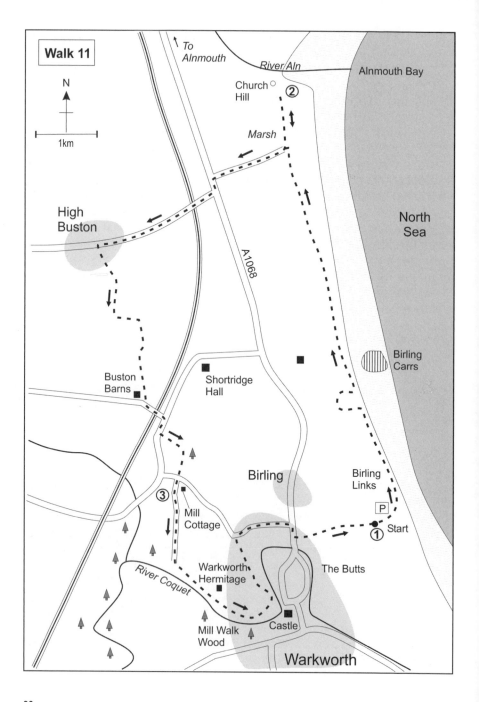

Church Hill is a historic and dramatic site with a large wooden cross at the top and beautiful views over the mouth of the River Aln to the pretty village of Alnmouth. Long ago, there was a Saxon church on the hill which was later replaced by a larger Norman church. Two pieces of a 10th century Saxon cross were dug up near the church in 1789. It is believed that the Anglo-Saxon settlement of Twyford was at Alnmouth. It was at the Synod of Twyford in AD684 that St Cuthbert was elected Bishop of Hexham, in his absence. The Northumbrian King Ecgfrith (the nephew of St Oswald of St Oswald's Way fame) was present at this event. In more recent times a Norman-like Mortuary Chapel was built at the foot of the hill in 1870 but this is now a picturesque ruin. The wooden cross on the hill is more recent still. In 1976, a rustic cross was erected to commemorate the centenary of the dedication of the Church of St John the Baptist, Alnmouth. Later in 1984, this was replaced by the current cross which was erected following an open air Diocesan service to celebrate the 1300th anniversary of the consecration of St Cuthbert as Bishop of Hexham. The service was led by the Bishop of Durham. The cross is known as St Cuthbert's Cross and was donated by the Duke of Northumberland.

The Mortuary Chapel on Church Hill

Alnmouth used to be a thriving port and was very prosperous during the 18th century. The river at this time flowed to the south of Church Hill (an area you have just crossed) but on Christmas day 1806, a violent storm changed the course of the river to its present state and the original harbour silted up. The remains of the church were also blown down.

2. When you have explored Church Hill, return over the marsh from the way you came and re-join the track at the metal gate. Turn right along the track to the main road (A1068), where you turn left at the roadside path. After About 100m turn right through a gap in the hedge, cross the road (take care) and go along the minor road (**High Buston 1, Shilbottle 3**). Follow the road all the way to High

Buston. Just after the postbox in the village turn left over a wall stile on to a footpath (**Buston Barns 1**). Go straight across the field to a wooden stile over a fence into a larger field, straight across to another wooden stile over a fence, and again across and down through some reeds and through a gate on to a bridleway. Go straight on across a clear path, through a stand of trees and through a gate into a large field. Follow the path along a line of telegraph poles. When you reach a metalled track across the path, turn left on to the public footpath. After about 200m turn sharp right towards Buston Barns and go through the Barns where you turn left on to a minor road. Go over a railway bridge and turn right at the junction. After about 200m turn left on to a footpath (**Mill Cottage ¼**) across a field. When you reach a small wood turn right towards Mill Cottage.

High Buston is a peaceful little place with some pleasant houses. High Buston Farm Cottage is the birthplace of John Common who became the blacksmith at Denwick near Alnwick. He contributed to the agricultural revolution by inventing a double-drill turnip sower and a reaping machine. Although this may sound rather comic, these machines were a great step forward in the labour-intensive days at the beginning of the 19th century. Other members of the Common family were famous for being very fit and strong and living to a very old age. One is said to have grown a new set of teeth a few years before he died at 110, and another entertained people by standing on his head on towers and church steeples and then lived to 115! They sound a real bunch of characters.

Near both High Buston and Low Buston are sites of medieval villages first recorded in 1242. Little remains of the one close to High Buston but the remains of the one at Low Buston is marked on the Ordnance Survey map and can still be made out with sunken roadways and enclosures. It is a Scheduled Monument protected by law and lies just beside Low Buston Hall.

3. You will see a sign near Mill Cottage with a map of the next section of the walk which is part of the DEFRA farm conservation scheme managed by Natural England. This is a glorious stretch along the River Coquet on the other side of the river to Warkworth Castle. The walk is open until 31st May 2020. If you are doing the walk after this date, you should check the DEFRA website to see if access

Warkworth Castle from the north bank of the River Coquet

has been extended. If permission has lapsed, turn left at the minor road at Mill Cottage, back to the A1068, then right and then left back to the start. The DEFRA walk has green waymarks, so go straight across the road past Mill Cottage and follow the track towards the trees down by the river with views of Warkworth Castle to the left. When you get to the woods, turn left following the green signs, go through a gate, across a field through another gate, cross a stile to your right and down a steep path towards the river. Cross a stile into a field and go half left towards a gate in the top right hand corner of the field. Go through the gate and follow the green signs along the river through another two gates. At the second of these gates, virtually directly opposite the castle, ignore the waymark pointing straight on and go half left away from the river on a more obvious path heading up a rise towards the top left hand corner of a fenced-off area of trees and bushes. At the cornerpost with a green waymark, go alongside the barbed-wire fence. Go through a wooden gate on your right in the field corner. You will see a house in front of you. Keeping close to the fence on your left at the top of the bank, follow the path round and after a short distance go through a gap in the fence and turn immediately right. **The waymark here is confusing as it implies you go straight on. The gap in the fence is before the house ahead, so if you find yourself between the house and the river, you should turn back and look for the gap at the top of the bank.** Go past some houses and come out on to a minor road where you turn right to reach the A1068. Turn right and then left along the road back to the car park.

For information about Warkworth, see Walk 16.

Walk 12: Clennell Street

This is a walk is in the upper reaches of Coquetdale and follows the River Alwin and White Burn through a deep valley to then climb up steeply to the tops and back along Clennell Street, an old drovers' road.

Distance	16.6km (10.3 miles)
Difficulty	Strenuous. There is one very steep ascent in the middle of the walk
Start	Grid Reference NT919063. Alwinton car park. Alwinton is 16km west of Rothbury on a minor road off the B6341
Parking	As above. The car park has toilets and also an electric car recharging point. In 2012 the parking fee was £2 for the whole day
Maps	OS 1:25000 Explorer OL16, the Cheviot Hills OS 1:50000 Landranger Sheet 80, Cheviot Hills & Kielder Forest area
Refreshments	Although Alwinton is small, it has its own pub, the Rose and Thistle, which provides food, drink and accommodation. Further afield, Rothbury has several places to stay, eat and drink
Advice	This walk is in the Cheviot Hills where it can get wet, extremely windy and visibility can be a challenge. In the winter the hills are likely to be covered in snow. Avoid adverse weather and come prepared. Do not attempt this walk after heavy rain as some of the fords over the White Burn may be impassable

200 years ago Alwinton was a much busier place than the quiet hamlet you find today. It was used as an overnight stop by Scottish cattle drovers. There was a blacksmith, a shoemaker, weavers and tailors and two pubs,

the Red Lion and the Rose and Thistle. The Rose and Thistle survives today and is understood to be the place where Sir Walter Scott stayed to gather material for his novel *Rob Roy*. Many towns and villages in Northumberland host annual shows (e.g. Powburn, Glanton, Bellingham, Harbottle). Alwinton is no exception and for the past 150 years has hosted the Border Shepherd's Show, the last in the season on the second Saturday in October. It is a fun day out with fell races, Cumberland and Westmoreland wrestling, stick dressing, pipe bands, dog trials, craft tents, beer tents and many other things.

1. Walk out of the car park and turn left past the Rose and Thistle and, where the road bends sharp right, go straight on over a patch of grass and cross a footbridge. Follow the restricted byway uphill (**Clennell Street, Border Ridge 8**) past a farm. After about 500m, at the end of a level stretch and before the path starts to climb, you will reach a ladder stile over a stone wall on your right, next to a metal gate. Go over this and follow the footpath along the edge of

The River Alwin in winter

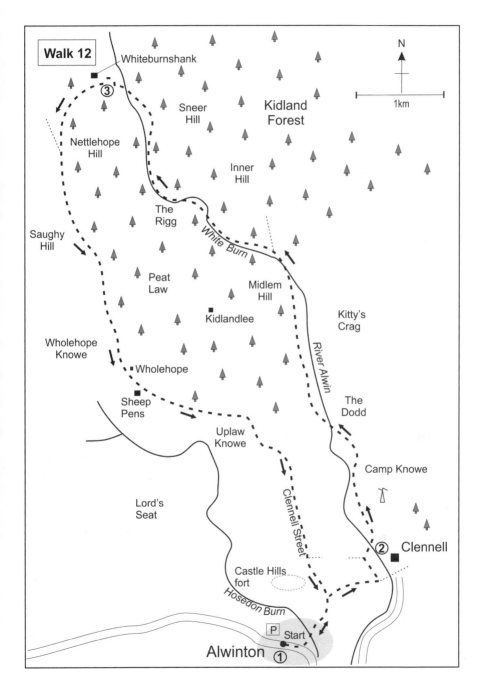

Walk 12

Whiteburnshank

③

Sneer
Hill

Kidland
Forest

Nettlehope
Hill

Inner
Hill

The
Rigg

White Burn

Saughy
Hill

Peat
Law

Midlem
Hill

Kitty's
Crag

Kidlandlee

River Alwin

Wholehope
Knowe

Wholehope

The
Dodd

Sheep
Pens

Uplaw
Knowe

Camp Knowe

Lord's
Seat

Clennell Street

② Clennell

Castle Hills
fort

Hosedon Burn

P Start

Alwinton ①

N

1km

the field to reach a metal gate into another field. Follow the indistinct path across the middle of this field to reach a stile, which you cross and follow the footpath signs downhill to a footbridge over the River Alwin. Cross the bridge just in front of Clennell Hall and turn left over a cattle grid along a broad track.

Clennell Hall is now a country hotel but was once an old pele-tower converted into a mansion house. It was the seat of the ancient Clennell family which dates back to Edward I (1239-1307). The nearby Church of St Michael and All Angels in Low Alwinton has an unusual crypt for the Clennell family. The chancel floor in this church was raised in the 14th Century so that it is separated from the nave by a flight of steps. The second step from the top can be lifted out and the rest can then follow to provide an entrance to the crypt underneath.

2. Go along the track and through a gate on to a private road (private for vehicles, not for walkers), and over a bridge. Follow the track for about 2.4km, keeping close to the river and crossing bridges, ignoring the footpath to your right (**Rookland 1, Puncherton 1¼**) to reach a wooded area. Ignore the bridleway back to Alwinton and the footpath to Kidlandlee, both to your left and enter the wooded area straight on through a gate. Follow the forest road for another 1.4km always following the river to reach the confluence of the River Alwin and the White Burn. Ignore the public bridleway going straight on and follow the footpath to your left over a footbridge where you immediately turn right along the water's edge through the trees to reach a forest track where you turn left along the White Burn. Follow the path for 3km crossing a number of fords. After the second ford, you reach a ruined sheepfold with a track off to your right. Do not take this but carry on along the main track along the burn to reach a concrete bridge with the building of Whiteburnshank visible up to your left. Cross the bridge and go straight on to the start of a very steep climb.

Whiteburnshank is an old farm building which has been converted into an outdoor centre. It is maintained by the Whiteburnshank Trust, a non profit making organization managed by a small group of volunteers. Thanks to a grant from the Sustainable Development Fund, they have installed a number of environmentally-friendly features, such as a wind turbine, photovoltaic cells and composting facilities. It is available for booking.

Clennell Street in winter

3. Keep on the main track uphill ignoring any paths off to the right
   to reach a wooden stile next to a gate with a path doubling back
   on you to the right. This is the Border County Ride, but you carry
   straight on along Clennell Street thankful that you are now on the
   homeward leg and the steep climb is now over. Walk straight on
   along the restricted byway (maroon coloured markers) ignoring
   any signs to the right or left and after about 2.4km you will see a
   ruined corrugated shack next to the older ruin of Wholehope.
   Where the main track bears sharp left, leave it and follow the
   restricted byway signs straight on to a grassy path. Go through a
   five-bar gate, pass the shack through a metal gate or over a stile
   and then pass the stone ruin of Wholehope. Go gently downhill to
   reach a stile by a metal gate with the Simonside Ridge visible ahead
   of you slightly to your left. Go through another gate towards some
   wooden enclosures (which are sheep pens) on your right. After the
   enclosures there is a narrow fork both prongs going uphill but
   with the right-hand one going to a higher point than the left-hand

one. Take the left-hand one, which is in effect going virtually straight on. When you get to the top of a rise, again the path splits. You will see a metal gate down below you to your left, but you should go on the less obvious of the two paths to your right towards some wooden gates by a small plantation. Go through the gate with a stile by the side of it and follow the path which after a short while descends downhill for about 3km all the way back to Alwinton.

Clennell Street is an old drovers' road between England and Scotland. For much of the way it coincides with the Border County Ride, a 100 mile circular route through Kielder Forest and the Cheviot Hills. It comes as a surprise to find out that Wholehope (pronounced locally as "Woolup") was a basic youth hostel between 1949 and the late 1960s when it fell into disrepair. It was demolished in the 1970s and there is really nothing left to show for it

Walk 13: Holystone

The Lady's Well and Dove Crag are the man-made and natural highlights of this walk and are visited on both the shorter and longer walks. If you want peace and tranquility in beautiful surroundings, this is the walk for you. Even the car park is a delight!

Distance	Full walk: 9.5km (5.9 miles) Shorter walk: 7.8km (4.8 miles)
Difficulty	Moderate
Start	Grid Reference NT950026. Holystone Forest Enterprise car park. To get to the start, take the B6341 through Rothbury and Thropton and turn right on to the minor road to Alwinton. Just after the bridge over the river at Sharperton turn left to Holystone. When you reach Holystone, follow the Forest Walks signs through the village to the Forest Enterprise Car Park
Parking	As above. In 2012, parking was free
Maps	OS 1:25000 Explorer OL16, the Cheviot Hills. The walk straddles OS 1:50000 Landranger Sheet 80, Cheviot Hills & Kielder Forest area and Sheet 81, Alnwick, Morpeth and surrounding area
Refreshments	There is nowhere to eat or drink in Holystone. There are two pubs in Thropton – the Three Wheat Heads and the Cross Keys. Rothbury is a lovely market town which has several tearooms, hotels and pubs
Advice	Some of this walk can be muddy in places, so come prepared with appropriate footwear. Parts of this walk cross fields with cattle in them. This is mainly a forest walk, so be prepared for midges and other flying insects in the summer months

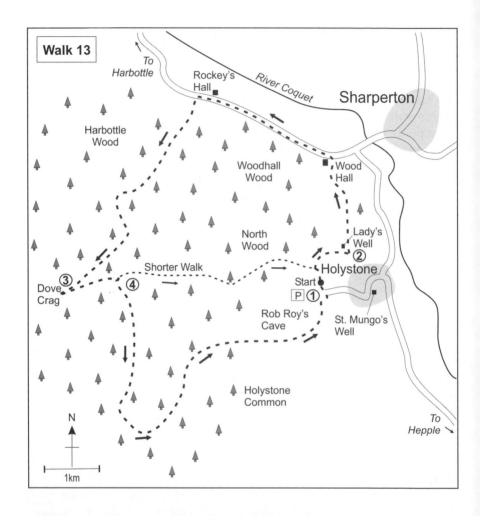

Walk 13

To Harbottle
Rockey's Hall
River Coquet
Sharperton
Harbottle Wood
Woodhall Wood
Wood Hall
North Wood
Lady's Well
②
Shorter Walk
Holystone
Start
③ Dove Crag
④
P ①
Rob Roy's Cave
St. Mungo's Well
Holystone Common
N
1km
To Hepple

There are three waymarked trails from the car park – red, orange and green. The red and orange colours on the waymarks are sometimes not easy to distinguish, so in these directions they are described as red/orange all the time. However, you should be aware that the trails have been known to change over time. The walks described here include parts of all three trails, but not necessarily in the intended directions.

1. The walk starts by following the green trail to the Lady's Well. From the information panel, enter the forest, go through a gate and

follow the track to reach a sign to the Lady's Well to the right. Follow the path to a kissing-gate into a field and head straight across to the well which is surrounded by a wicket fence on a stone wall. Follow the wall and turn back on yourself to enter the serene enclosure.

The Lady's Well is a Grade I listed National Trust site. It is unattended and free to enter. It gets its name from the 12th Century when a priory of Augustinian nuns was established in Holystone. But it goes back much further than that. It was used as a watering place on a Roman Road linking Bremenium (at Rochester in Northumberland) with Dere Street. It is also called St Ninian's Well after the 6th Century Scottish bishop who may have visited the site. The well is a beautiful, tranquil basin surrounded by beech trees and fed by a natural spring. In the centre of the pool is a large stone wheel cross with an inscription: "In this place Paulinus the Bishop baptised 3000 Northumbrians, Easter DCXXVII". However, according to Tomlinson's *Comprehensive Guide to Northumberland*, on this Easter Day in AD627,

The Lady's Well

Paulinus was actually at St Peter's Church in York. In Latin, Holystone is *Sancta Petra* and St Peter's is *Sancti Petri*, and over time this is where the confusion seems to have come from. Nevertheless, it is believed there may be some truth in the occasion, even though the date may be inaccurate. At one end of the pool is a 15th century statue of St Paulinus, and at the

Coins on the Holy Stone

other end is a stone altar, the Holy Stone, on which visitors have taken to leaving coins.

2. Come out of the well, turn left following the footpath round to reach two fields where you enter the one on the right. Walk along the edge of the field with the hedge on your left, and go over a stile into a narrow stretch of land to a squeeze stile, following the yellow waymarks. Head straight across another field going slightly downhill to reach a stile and follow the path along the right-hand edge of a field to another stile. Head up the track towards Wood Hall. Go through a gate on to the road and turn left. Follow the road for about 1.3km, taking care as there is no pavement, to reach two houses on your right (Rockey's Hall and Lightpipe Hall). Turn left off the road on to a restricted byway (**High Shaw 4¼**) into the forest. This is a broad red track which you follow for just over 1.5 km as it rises uphill through the forest, following the purple restricted byway signs and ignoring any footpaths off to the right and left. The track eventually reaches the top of the rise and levels out. About 100m after this, as the path sweeps round to the left, take the footpath to the right across a little wooden plank bridge into the forest. This is a pleasant path through the trees with yellow waymarks which joins another path and then eventually meets a broader path which you follow to the right. After a few metres you reach a small clearing where the path splits, the footpath going straight on and Dove Crag visible to your right. Go to the right and turn right off the track into Dove Crag itself, making your way towards the idyllic waterfall.

Dove Crag comes upon you by surprise. It is a sandstone canyon with a pretty waterfall where the Dovecrag Burn tumbles over the far end and is

a lovely place for a picnic. One can imagine it being the haunt of fairies. Here is an extract from David Dippie Dixon's wonderful book *Upper Coquetdale, Northumberland: its history, traditions, folk-lore and scenery*, published in 1903: "in days gone by, this was reputed to be one of the favourite haunts of the Fairies, and stories were told by the country folk of belated travellers when near the spot at the 'witching time of night' having been spell-bound by the sweet entrancing music of the little elves, while in the midst of their midnight revels at the foot of the Dove Crag." There is a small fir tree near the waterfall which, in 2011, had been decorated for Christmas by an imaginative visitor.

3. When you have finished visiting the crag, retrace your steps back through the clearing and on a few metres to the fork where you joined the broader path from out of the forest and, instead of turning left from where you came, go straight on through the trees along the broader path for nearly 500m to reach the red restricted byway again. This is where you can either complete the shorter walk or continue with the full walk. For the full walk, go to Paragraph 4. For the shorter walk, go straight across the red track on to another broad red track, actually doing the red/orange route in reverse. Follow straight on with a wire fence on your left. The red track gives way to a grassy track with the fence still to your left. When the fence bends round to the left, carry straight on towards North Wood. Enter the oak wood and when you reach a marker post, turn left at the fork and follow the path through the wood, dropping down. When you reach the corner of a field, turn right and follow the field edge, going downhill all the way. When you reach another field corner, go straight into the woods through a couple of stone gateposts, to reach the track on which you started, where you turn right back to the car park.

North Wood, managed by the Forestry Commission, is a sessile oak wood which has survived since at least 1600. It is rare to find such a wood in Northumberland, being more characteristic of the Lake District. In Elizabethan times so many oak trees were being felled for fuel and building that a law was introduced protecting the oak as it was needed for the construction of ships. After that, oaks were commonly coppiced and there is evidence of this practice in North Wood. It is a Site of Special Scientific Interest. It is a delightful experience to walk through this wood in Autumn.

Dove Crag

4. For the full walk, turn right on to the red track when you come out of the forest. When you reach a fork, do not follow the track round to the left but go straight on in a southerly direction along the restricted byway (which is still quite broad). Eventually as you approach the edge of the forest and as the track bends slightly to the right, you will reach a clear path cut into the bank going left off the track which you follow for a short distance through some trees, coming out on to open ground and leading straight across a metalled road to a finger-post (**Restricted Byway, High Shaw 2½**) across more open ground and into the woods. Walk downhill along this path to the bottom of a valley where you will find a multi-waymarked post. Turn left along a footpath (a broad track) with Holystone Burn down to your right. When you reach a marker post pointing straight ahead off the track, ignore this and continue on the main track all the way back to the metalled road, where you turn right and walk for over 1km back to the car park.

Sir Walter Scott's novel, *Rob Roy*, seems to have had an influence on the area. On the Ordnance Survey map (OL16) can be found Rob Roy's Cave near the car park in a deep gorge of the Dovecrag Burn. It does not now seem to be accessible to the public. St Mungo's Well can also be found on the map and this is by the roadside between Holystone and the car park. St Mungo (or Kentigern) was a Celtic missionary and is the patron saint of Glasgow. He is said to have passed through Holystone on his way from St Asaph (in Wales) to Glasgow. However, locally this used to be called the Mugger's Well (mugger being the local word for tinker) and the name St Mungo's only seems to have appeared after the publication of *Rob Roy* in which Scott describes St Mungo's Church in Glasgow. An intriguing derivation if ever there was one, which may or may not be true.

Walk 14: Simonside Hills

This is a popular hill walk among hikers in Northumberland. It goes from the pretty town of Rothbury high up along the Simonside Ridge with spectacular views to the north. It descends through woods and back along the River Coquet.

Distance	12.7km (7.9 miles)
Difficulty	Strenuous. There are some serious ascents and descents to and from the Simonside Ridge
Start	Grid Reference NU057015. The car park by the river in Rothbury. As you enter the town on the B6344 from the east, turn left over the bridge and then right at a junction. The car park is a short distance along on the right
Parking	As above. In 2012, the parking fee was 20p per hour
Maps	OS 1:25000 Explorer OL42, Kielder Water & Forest; OS 1:50000 Landranger Sheet 81, Alnwick, Morpeth and surrounding area
Refreshments	There are several places in Rothbury which provide accommodation, food and drink
Advice	This is a ridge walk. It can get wet, extremely windy and visibility can be a challenge. Avoid adverse weather and come prepared

Rothbury is a pleasant traditional town on the banks of the River Coquet and is known as the capital of Coquetdale. There are plenty of shops, cafes and pubs and it is a popular base for walkers and cyclists. Close by is the magnificent Cragside Estate, the former home of Lord Armstrong, and now in the care of the National Trust. It is a very popular tourist attraction and in June the grounds are awash with the colour of rhododendrons. Lord Armstrong was a Victorian engineer, inventor and entrepreneur and the house was the first in the world to be powered by hydro-electricity. The gardens are a real treat with one of the largest rock gardens in Europe. It is a lovely place to visit.

In July 2010, Rothbury was the scene of the closing stages of the largest manhunt in modern British history. The peace of the town was shattered when Raoul Moat, who had recently been released from Durham Prison, was cornered on the banks of the river after seriously wounding his ex-girlfriend, killing her partner and then shooting a police officer. He had been on the run for a week, living rough in Northumberland until he was finally surrounded in Rothbury. In the stand-off Moat shot himself and died from his injuries.

1. Walk out of the car park and turn right along the road going uphill past Rothbury Community Hospital and the Golf Club. At the road junction, turn left (**Whitton ½**) still climbing past Whitton Tower and just before the top of the rise take the path on your right between **Woodfold Juniper** and **Hill Cottage**. Pass **Sharp's Folly** on your right, ignore the first footpath by a metal gate to your left, and when the path splits, take the bridleway left (**Whittondean ¼, Lordenshaw Fort 1**).

Sharp's Folly is the oldest folly in the county and was built by the Rev Thomas Sharp who was the Rector of Rothbury between 1720 and 1758. He built it as an observatory but also as a sort of job creation scheme for unemployed local stonemasons.

2. When you get to a farm, go through the gate signed **public footpath only**, pass the farm on your left, and then turn immediately right following the footpath signs. Walk along the stony path

Sharp's Folly

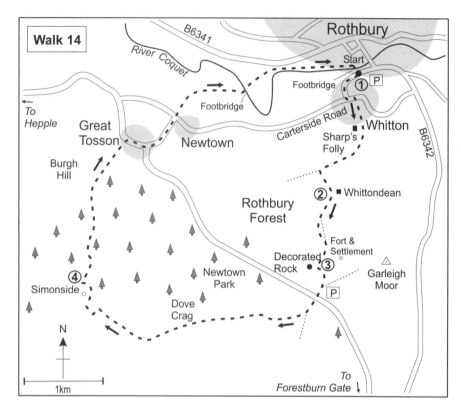

past some wooden chalets, cross the burn and turn right off the main track along a grassy path to a metal gate and a stile. Follow the footpath and St Oswald's Way markers as the path turns left, and climb uphill past some hawthorn trees to reach a broken-down stone wall which you go through and bear half-right. Carry on uphill and at a crossroad of paths visit the cup and ring marked rock off to your right. Return from this Ancient Monument back to the crossroads. If you go straight across the crossroads, you will reach the Lordenshaws Iron Age hillfort up ahead of you.

Lordenshaws is an Iron Age hillfort, circular in form and protected by three sets of ramparts and ditches. Within the central enclosure are the remains of seven round houses. Many of the rocks around the fort are carved with cup and ring markings and the site is thought to have the greatest concentration of such rocks in the county.

3. When you have finished head back to the crossroads and follow the marker posts to a large parking area to the south by a road. Go through the car park, across the road and take the footpath up the hill (**Spylaw 1¼, Coquet Cairn 2½**) to reach a fork where you turn right away from St Oswald's Way towards the ridge. Climb to the **Beacon Cairn** where the clear path levels out for a good distance until you reach a wooden gate and then climb some stone steps to the cairn on **Dove Crag**, ignoring the red waymark to the right just before the cairn. Follow the clear flagged path along the ridge to **Old Stell Crag** which you reach at the top of some steps. Continue along the path to **Simonside** the high point at 430m and the end of the ridge. Some say this is the best view in Northumberland with the Cheviot Hills across Coquetdale to the north-west and the coast to the east. From Simonside continue along the edge of the ridge to a very steep path going downhill to a forest track. You will have to pick your way down here very carefully.

The origin of the name Simonside is unclear. If it is named after a Simon, then no-one knows for sure who he was, although there are suggestions that he was a domestic brewer to King Arthur! It has also been suggested that it comes from "seaman's sight" as the hills can be seen from the sea, but this seems rather far-fetched. The Simonside Hills are also said to be haunted by the Duergar, a race of mischievous elves who delight in leading unwary travellers astray, especially after dark, into dangerous and boggy terrain.

4. At the bottom, turn right along the track and, ignoring the marker post on your right, you will reach a marker post on your left after a short distance. The post has arrows on the opposite side to where you are coming from, so you will have to keep your eyes peeled for this. Turn left across a short stretch of heath towards the forest. After entering the trees, turn right along a footpath crossing your way, and follow this downhill and across another path, following the footpath signs and the orange trail. When you reach a forest drive on the edge of the forest, turn right and very quickly turn left through a gate, leaving the orange trail behind. The views over open fields are really lovely, almost alpine. Go along the grassy path and over a ladder stile on a stone wall, then through the next field and over a stile near a gate. Where the path splits take the right-hand fork downhill alongside a stone wall. At the end of the wall, work your way downhill towards Great Tosson below you on your right

View north from the Simonside Ridge

going through a kissing-gate and over a stile, and turn right into the village. Join the road straight on through the village past the remains of Tosson Tower, a 15th Century ruin whose walls are over 2 metres thick, and at the fork in the road, turn left downhill to a junction. Turn left, go round a bend and take the minor road to the right (**Tosson Mill ¼**). After the buildings, the little road becomes an unsurfaced track which soon turns sharp right and goes alongside a hedge and a wire fence for about 600m to reach the Lady's Bridge over the River Coquet. Cross the bridge, go through a kissing-gate into a field and follow the footpath (**Rothbury 1**) towards the B6344 road. On the other side of the field cross a small footbridge, go up a small bank through a kissing-gate and turn right along a well-laid sand-coloured path. Follow this path all the way along the river for about 1.25km, ignoring the footbridge to the golf course, eventually meeting another footbridge back across the river to the car park.

Tosson Tower

Walk 15: Weldon Bridge

This walk is from Weldon Bridge to Felton along the beautiful River Coquet. Part of the walk follows a Natural England permissive access path and access ends in July 2017. An alternative route is provided for walks after this date. There is a shorter and longer version of the walk.

Distance	Full walk: 14.3km (8.9 miles) Shorter walk: 7.7km (4.8 miles)
Difficulty	Moderate. There are a couple of short sharp climbs but it is flat nearly all the way
Start	Grid reference NZ138985. Weldon Bridge – outside the Anglers Arms. Turn off the A697 on to the B6344 to Rothbury. Virtually immediately turn left on to a minor road and the Anglers Arms is a short distance along
Parking	You should find space to park for free. The Anglers Arms also has a car park
Maps	OS 1:25000 Explorer 325, Morpeth & Blyth OS 1:50000 Landranger Sheet 81, Alnwick, Morpeth and surrounding area and Sheet 75, Berwick-upon-Tweed and surrounding area
Refreshments	The Anglers Arms is a great pub. It has several rooms to stay in and serves good food all day
Advice	Some of this walk can be muddy in places, so come prepared with appropriate footwear. Part of the return walk is along a Natural England Permissive Access Path and access officially ends on 31 July 2017. So, if you are doing the walk after this date, you should check out whether it is still open. If not, you can miss out this stretch and return along the path you took on the outward leg

1. From the Anglers Arms go back up the minor road to the junction with the B6344. At the junction turn immediately right, cross over the road and follow the sign for St Oswald's Way walking along the verge. Go under the A697 and follow the road round taking a track on your left through a wooden gate again signed St Oswald's Way. After about 500m you reach Low Weldon. Follow the bridleway round to the left and round the back of the house. Carry on to reach High Weldon where you will find some holiday cottages. Carry straight on through the buildings along a paved path, ignoring the road that goes off to the left, and continue along the bridleway. The path bears right through a gate and then gradually descends to a wooden gate on to an open field. Follow the path to the Catheugh Estate alongside the River Coquet. Go through the gate to the left of the cattle grid at the entrance and follow the bridleway up and round the back of the house. After a dip (which can get very muddy and slippery) go through a wooden gate. Ignore the kissing-gate to the left (a Natural England permissive access path) and also ignore the erroneous signs indicating St Cuthbert's Way which is much further north (you are still, in fact, on St Oswald's Way). Carry on through the woods with the river down to your right to reach a wooden railing.

The Anglers Arms at Weldon Bridge is a famous old inn built in the 1760s. It has an old-world charm and is full of interesting memorabilia. It has a private one-mile stretch of the River Coquet available to guests wishing to fish for brown trout and seasonal runs of sea trout and salmon. It is next to an elegant Grade I listed, three-arched bridge over the River Coquet, with circular openings between the arches to allow water to flow through when the river is high. The current bridge replaced older bridges which were destroyed by floods in the middle of the 18th Century. The Coquet is liable to flooding and, in the bad floods of 2008, the river entered the cellars of the Anglers Arms.

The Anglers Arms at Weldon Bridge

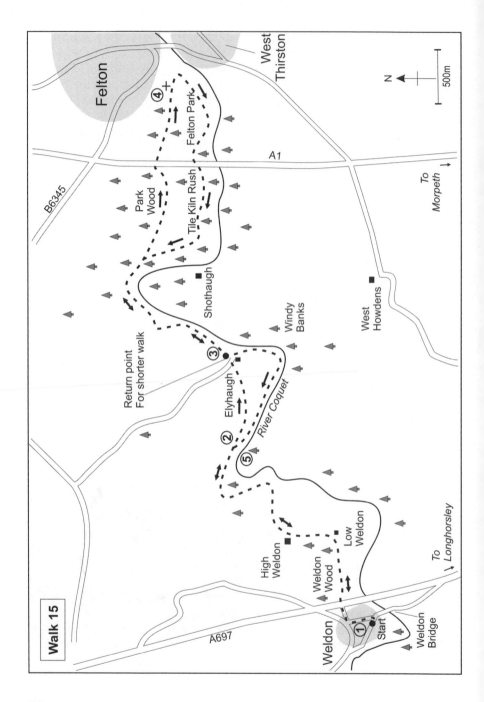

Walk 15

West Thirston

Felton

Felton Park

Park Wood

Tile Kiln Rush

B6345

A1

To Morpeth

N

500m

Shothaugh

Return point
For shorter walk

Windy Banks

West Howdens

Elyhaugh

River Coquet

High Weldon

Weldon Wood

Low Weldon

Weldon

A697

Weldon Bridge

Start

To Longhorsley

St Oswald's Way is one of several long-distance paths which cross parts of Northumberland. It goes from Heavenfield near Hadrian's Wall to Holy Island and links places associated with St Oswald, a 7th Century King of Northumbria, who played a major part in introducing Christianity to the area. Stretches of other long-distance paths which feature in this book are The Hadrian's Wall Path (Walk 25), St Cuthbert's Way (Walk 3), The Pennine Way (Walk 28), the South Tyne Trail (Walk 26) and the Northumberland Coastal Path (Walks 2, 6, 7, 11 and 16).

2. There is a Natural England path straight on, on which we shall be returning, but for now, ignore it and turn left through a gate along the bridleway. Go along the field edge through a gate into another field and go across this field, bearing slightly left towards a metal gate with a stile to its left. Cross over and follow the track (often muddy) along the edge of the field and across a smaller field passing to the left of a very large tree stump to reach a house (Elyhaugh). Go through a gate just in front of the house, turn slightly left and through another gate signed **Access to the River**. Go round the house, left down a bank and right towards the river where you will find a gate and a stile on to the river bank. *For the short walk do not go through the gate but return to the start by turning right just before the burn past the house (go to paragraph 5)*.

Elyhaugh is a fine, Grade II listed house built in 1732 for the Lisle family. It has been added to since that date. Early maps indicate the presence of an orchard and a well but these are no longer evident on the ground. The house is also thought to be on the site of a medieval village.

3. Again ignore the Natural England path to the right. Go left along the river bank for about 200m to a stile where you take the footpath to the right signed **Felton Fence ¾, Felton 2**. Carry on along the river looking out for herons which are commonly found round here. Head to the right of two ash trees at the top of a rise with a stile in between them. Before you reach the trees go through a gate to the right of them with a footpath sign. Drop down towards the river following the waymarks, cross a wooden footbridge, up a slight rise and on towards a gate on to a wooden footbridge into a wood. Turn right after the bridge towards the river and follow the path until you reach a fork where you take the less obvious path to the left. Go over a stile into a very long field, heading towards

the top right-hand corner, passing a stone barn half way along. Near the top of the field there is a quaint cottage to the left with a tarred track leading to it. Turn right on to this and follow it round and down under the A1. Continue on this track and as it sweeps round past some farm buildings, go straight on to the footpath into a wood. Follow the path through the woods and down where you will meet a broad track across your path. Turn right here along the footpath. Follow the path to a metalled road and turn left and past the Church of St Michael and All Angels, although you may wish to visit this church as it is very interesting.

The Church of St Michael and All Angels is approached along a lavender-lined path and has been in existence since the late 12th Century, with the nave and the chancel being the oldest parts. Now, it is one of the four largest churches in Northumberland. The church is notable for, among other things, its very flat roof, its large and primitive bell-cote and the beautiful window in the east end of the south aisle. The head of the

The Church of St Michael and All Angels, Felton

window is cut from one piece of sandstone and has lovely geometric tracery made up of circular figures. There is no other design like it in Northumberland. It is well worth having a good look round the church and its grounds. There are some very informative panels inside the porch.

4. After the church turn right on to the footpath signed **Felton Fence 1¾**. Go through a kissing-gate into Felton Park. Walk along the pleasant grassy track with the river down to your left and through a kissing-gate into a wood. Go along the top of a steep gorge to a gate just before the A1. Take the steps down, go under the A1 and up the other side to a gate. Go through the gate and follow the path straight on. Follow the path all the way back through the woods to meet the marker post where you originally branched off. Go straight on and drop down to the left towards the river when the path splits again towards the footbridge where you entered the wood on the outward leg. From here re-trace your steps to Elyhaugh along the river. Go back through the metal gate or over the stile just in front of Elyhaugh next to the river and then cross a burn and turn left immediately past the bottom of the house. **This is a Natural England Permissive Access Path and access officially ends on 31 July 2017. If you are doing the walk after this date and the path is no longer accessible you should re-trace your steps from Paragraph 3 back to the beginning.**

This access has been provided under the Department for Environment, Food & Rural Affairs' farm conservation schemes and is managed by Natural England. These schemes have opened up previously inaccessible parts of the country to the public. Some of these, such as this stretch along the River Coquet, are really beautiful and, if lucky, you can sight otters and red squirrels. The schemes are intended to help farmers improve the countryside, its wildlife and history. There is a time limit to each of these schemes – this one expires in 2017. After these dates, the access ends, but one can live in hope! Other such schemes used in this book are in Chillingham Park (Walk 4) and the north side of the River Coquet in Warkworth (Walk 11). Both of these are absolute treasures.

5. If you are returning on the longer walk, turn left just over the burn, between the house and the river. If you are doing the shorter walk, turn right just before the burn between the house and the river. Cross a wooden footbridge following the green Natural England

signs. This stretch of the river is absolutely gorgeous. Go through a kissing-gate on the banks of the river, then another kissing-gate and then another right into a field. Go along the field edge, through two gates to reach a kissing-gate into a wood. Follow the path over a wooden footbridge, going up and down along the path crossing another footbridge, eventually reaching a gap in a fence where you originally branched off. From here, re-trace your steps back to the start from Paragraph 2.

Walk 16: Low Hauxley

This is a wonderful walk starting from Low Hauxley Nature Reserve, along the north of Druridge Bay to Amble at the mouth of the River Coquet. It then leads to the pretty town of Warkworth with its wonderful Castle and follows the Coquet around the back of it. It returns over fields to Low Hauxley.

Distance	17.8km (11.1 miles)
Difficulty	Moderate. A longish walk but easy going
Start	Grid Reference NU282024 Hauxley Nature Reserve. Going north on the A1068, turn right after Radcliffe to High Hauxley. After a sharp right hand bend, there is a short stretch of road and then a sharp left-hand bend. At this bend, go straight on off the main road to the Hauxley Nature Reserve. There are some very wicked speed bumps here! When the road bears left to the Caravan Park, turn right along a track to the Nature Reserve car park
Parking	In 2012, parking was free
Maps	OS 1:25000 Explorer 332, Alnwick & Amble; OS 1:50000 Landranger Sheet 81, Alnwick, Morpeth and surrounding area
Refreshments	There are plenty of places to eat and drink in Amble and Warkworth
Advice	If you can arrange it, try to start this walk at low tide, to take full advantage of the wonderful beach. Bring your binoculars to view the birds in the Nature Reserve. Warkworth Castle is open all year round (but not every day in the winter months). The Hermitage is only open on certain days of the week and not at all in the winter months. It would be wise to check beforehand

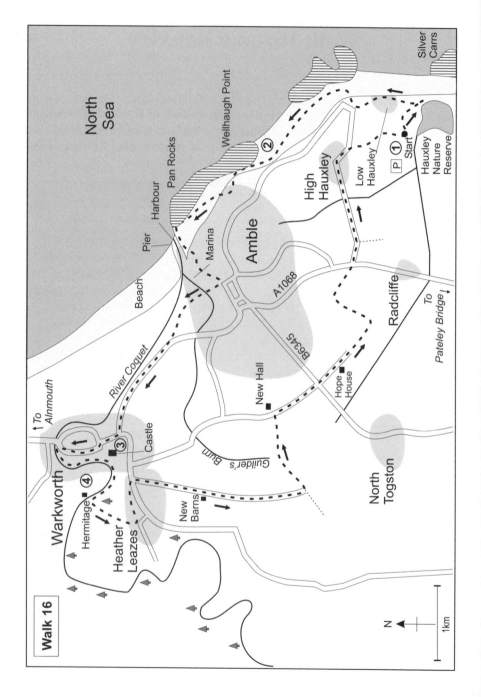

Walk 16

North Sea

Silver Carrs

Wellhaugh Point

Pan Rocks

Harbour

Pier

Beach

Marina

Amble

High Hauxley

Low Hauxley

Hauxley Nature Reserve

Start

P ①

②

A1068

B6345

New Hall

Hope House

Radcliffe

To Pateley Bridge ↓

North Togston

River Coquet

To Alnmouth ↑

Castle

Warkworth

Hermitage

Heather Leazes

New Barns

Guilder's Burn

③

④

N

1km

112

Hauxley Nature Reserve is managed by Northumberland Wildlife Trust. Like many nature reserves in the area it is a reclaimed open cast coal mining site. In June 2010 the main reception building was burned down by vandals on the night that England was knocked out of the World Cup by Germany in South Africa, but there are plans to re-build it and a temporary one is open next to the Warden's Office. It is a great place for birdwatching as there are several bird hides. The information panels are particularly interesting, especially the one about local flora. It describes 11 plants, and includes the traditional ways in which they were used. For example, kidney vetch is so called because of its use in the treatment of kidney problems and viper's bugloss cures the bite of a viper!

1. Enter the Nature Reserve near the Warden's Office and bear left past the information boards along a cinder track. There are a number of bird hides here which you may like to visit. Follow the track round to a footpath to the left signposted **Coastal Route Ponteland Hide**. Turn left here, go through a gate and then immediately turn left along the Coastal Route to Low Hauxley (signposted). Go through a gate with a National Cycle Network No. 1 sign on it. As you approach Low Hauxley you can see Coquet Island coming into view on your right. Low Hauxley is very small but you may wish to have a look around it with its pretty square. Follow the road through the village to a junction with a number of wooden beach houses by the road. Turn right (signposted **Amble**) and right again after the telephone box through a gap in the fence on to the beach. Head north up the beach and as you turn the corner you will see the wonderful Northumberland coastline stretching ahead of you, with Dunstanburgh Castle in the farthest right hand corner of the view. As Coquet Island lines up directly to your right, keep your eyes on the sand beneath you, and you will see wood coming out of the sand – the remains of tree trunks and branches from an ancient forest which used to be here before the sea took over.

Low Hauxley is a pleasant little village and was built in the 1850s. It became a thriving fishing community and had a lifeboat station until 1939. However, people have been living in the area since 6500 BC and in 1983 a bronze age burial cist containing a male skeleton from around 1700 BC was revealed after a winter storm. At this time, the sea would have been a mile further east and the cist would have been part of a burial cairn.

Coquet Islalnd

Coquet Island is an RSPB reserve which is home to large colonies of nesting seabirds including roseate terns and eider ducks. The public are not allowed to land on the island. The island was used as a monastic cell in the 7th century and much later as a lighthouse station. In fact Grace Darling's elder brother, William, was the first lighthouse keeper.

2. Head up the beach towards a house straight ahead of you with a white gable end. You will pass this house soon. Before the beach starts to sweep round to the right, there is a stretch of dunes which are not as high as those surrounding them. Head left here into the dunes where there are plenty of sandy paths. At the top of the dunes, you will see a caravan park on the other side of a road ahead of you. Turn right on to a path running parallel with the road and follow it to the white house. Go through a kissing-gate, past the house and car park. Stick to the path until you come to a stretch of green. Follow the top end of the green towards a churchyard, then

follow the path round the churchyard alongside the boundary wall. Carry on past some houses on your left and then a playground area. Head towards the top of the green keeping the playground to your right, and then go on to the pier straight ahead. Follow the pier into the middle of the River Coquet, then turn sharp left up the river. Keep a lookout for water birds, in particular the eider duck, which is native to the area. At the end of the pier head straight on through the harbour yard. At the end of the yard is a harbour inlet where eider ducks often congregate. Go on to the road (Leazes Street), and follow it round into Amble. Go along Queen Street and turn right at North Street to a large green (The Braid). Follow the track straight on past Amble Marina, then keeping to the side of the river, pass Coquet Yacht Club and as you round the corner you will see the magnificent Warkworth Castle ahead. Walk past Amble Boat Club on to a green, go straight across on to the road (A1068) and follow the road for about 1¼km along the river into Warkworth. At the top of the road, turn right at the junction (signed **Alnwick** and **Alnmouth**) towards the Castle.

The eider duck is the UK's heaviest and fastest flying duck. The down from the duck is called eiderdown, giving the name to the bed-covering. Locally it is known as "Cuddy's Duck" after St Cuthbert who gave them sanctuary on the Farne Islands in the 7th century. The males have an unusual and rather humorous "crooning" call, rather like a human expressing surprise.

Male eider duck in Amble Harbour

3. The castle is an English Heritage site and is open to the public. After the castle, follow the road into Warkworth where there are plenty of tearooms and pubs. At the end of the town as the road turns right and over a bridge, you will see a gatehouse on your left. Turn left just before the archway and follow the footpath (**Monk's Walk, Coast Path**) along the river for nearly 1½km, keeping to the river all the time. You

will pass St Lawrence's Church, some picnic tables and pass below the Castle. You will come to a gate leading on to an open grassy space. If you have come on the right day, you can take the boat across the river to Warkworth Hermitage, a magical place.

Warkworth is a very attractive town built on a loop of the River Coquet. The Castle, which is now a ruin, defended approaches from the south while a fortified bridge defended the north. The Castle and Hermitage are both managed by English Heritage and are open to the public. The Castle is known for its wonderful cross-shaped keep. It was once the home of the Percy family and the Duke of Northumberland still owns it but now lives in Alnwick Castle. The Hermitage is accessed by ringing a bell on the bank of the River Coquet which alerts a boatman to come and ferry you across. It dates back to the 14th century and there are a number of legends associated with it. The most dramatic of these is that the Hermitage was founded by a knight, Sir Bertram, who carved it out of the rock after mistakenly killing his lover and his brother as he tried to rescue her from the Scots. People passing by are said to have heard the hermit's howls of anguish as he begged forgiveness for his deed. It truly is an exquisite place with nothing else like it in the country. St Lawrence's Church is also worth

Warkworth Castle from Amble

mentioning as many original Norman features still remain, the nave being the longest in Northumberland.

Warkworth Hermitage

4. Go left up the hill away from the river and Hermitage along a path which soon becomes a metalled road. At the junction, turn left, and just before another junction, take the footpath left (**Warkworth Castle ½ mile**). The path goes behind some houses and where it bears left towards the Castle, turn right through a cut between two houses. At the road turn left and after a short stretch (less than 100m) turn right opposite the house addressed Number 1. Carry on along the road in the direction of a large water tower and follow the track towards New Barns Farm. Go along the tarmacced road after the farm for just over 1km and as the road sweeps right take the bridleway left. After another 1km go through a metal gate to another metal gate on to a road with a house straight in front of you. Turn right on to the road and follow it for ½km to a crossroads. Go straight across towards a farm (**Hope House**). Pass the farm buildings on your right and some holiday cottages on your left, and as the tarmac finishes, go straight on along a track. The track goes straight on for ¾km, turns sharp left for about ½km and then sharp right for another ½km, passing through a number of metal and then wooden gates. It comes out on to the A1068, which you cross and follow the road all the way back for 2km through High Hauxley and on to the Nature Reserve.

Walk 17: Kielder – Duke and Duchess Trail

This walk together with Walk 18 makes a figure of eight walk, with Kielder Castle in the middle. They can be done separately or in one go. This walk goes into the Forest near Kielder Castle and then visits an arboretum from where it returns to the start.

Distance	4.8km (3.0 miles)
Difficulty	Easy
Start	Grid Reference NY632937. Kielder Castle Visitor Centre car park
Parking	The car park is next to Kielder Castle at the northern end of Kielder Water off the C200, the road which goes along the southern edge of the reservoir. In 2012 the parking fee was £4 per day but, once bought, the ticket is valid for all car parks round the reservoir
Maps	OS 1:25000 Explorer OL42, Kielder Water & Forest; OS 1:50000 Landranger Sheet 80, Cheviot Hills & Kielder Forest area
Refreshments	The Duke's Pantry tearoom at the Forestry Commission's Kielder Castle Visitor Centre is open all year round. Northumbrian Water has a couple of Visitor Centres on the reservoir at Tower Knowe and Leaplish but the restaurant opening times are seasonal. There is a youth hostel in Kielder Village. The Angler's Arms in Kielder Village provides accommodation and there are very good pubs at the eastern end of the reservoir which also provide accommodation – the Blackcock Country Inn at Falstone and the Pheasant Inn at Stannersburn
Advice	Kielder Water is notorious for its midges – small irritating flying insects which bite. They appear

Advice (cont'd)	at the end of May and disappear in September. So, if you are doing the walk at this time, insect repellant is a good idea. Make sure you have plenty of petrol as there are very few petrol stations in the immediate vicinity and, as it is a remote area, petrol is expensive

Kielder Water was opened by Queen Elizabeth II in 1982. It is the largest man-made lake in Northern Europe and is surrounded by the largest working forest in England. It was designed by Sir Frederick Gibberd (1908 -1984), the architect and town planner, whose other notable achievements include Harlow New Town, the original Heathrow Terminal 2 (closed in 2009) and the wonderful Roman Catholic Cathedral in Liverpool. The construction of Kielder Water was not without controversy. It was planned in the 1960s to satisfy an expected increase in demand for water by heavy industry in the North-East such as ICI and British Steel. As we all know, heavy industry declined rather than grew leading some critics to label it as a white elephant or "the largest boating lake in Europe"! However, in recent years it has proved valuable to the area with the North-East having plentiful supplies of water and the south of England experiencing hose-pipe bans. It is also one of Northumberland's biggest tourist attractions. Whatever your views, it is a great place for outdoor pursuits whether it be walking, sailing or mountain-biking.

1. Walk out of the car park and down to the Visitor Centre where you will find a very large finger post with all the trails on it. From the post walk to the right of the Visitor Centre to a sign for the Duchess

Kielder Reservoir

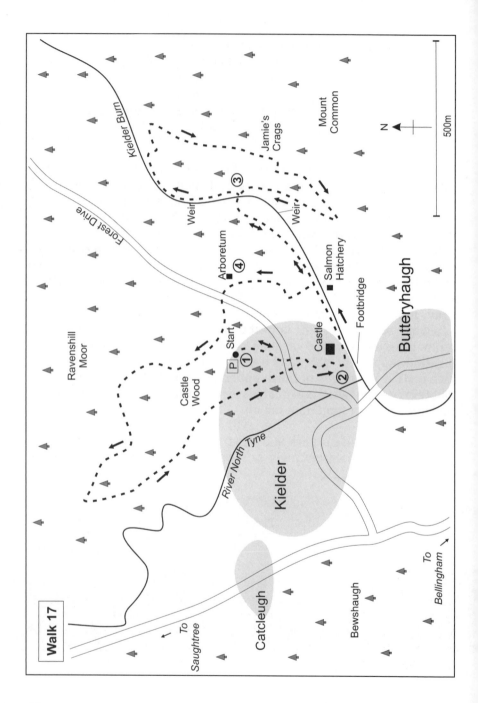

Walk 17

Kielder Burn

Mount Common

Jamie's Crags

N

500m

Forest Drive

Weir

Weir

③

Arboretum

④

Salmon Hatchery

Footbridge

Ravenshill Moor

Castle Wood

P Start

①

Castle

②

Butteryhaugh

River North Tyne

Kielder

Catcleugh

Bewshaugh

To Saughtree

To Bellingham

Trail (green waymarks) and the Minotaur Maze.

The area around Kielder water has become the largest open air art and architecture gallery in the country. In the next walk is the Skyspace installation. On this walk we have the Minotaur Maze, designed by Nick Coombe and Shona Kitchen in 2003. The final goal in the maze is a small room which shines with rocks made from recycled glass. It is popular with adults and children alike. There are several other installations around the lake.

The Minotaur Maze

2. Drop down some steps through a gap in a fence passing the maze on your right to reach the Kielder Burn where you turn left. Follow the green arrows of the Duchess Trail along the bank of the burn. When the path forks, take the right side through a gate into a field and head towards a stone bridge next to a weir over the burn. On the other side of the bridge, turn left down some steps and walk along the burn. After a while, the path bears away from the burn into the forest, and very soon you meet a cinder track where you turn left going slightly uphill. You will reach a bench with a lovely view over the burn where you do a U-turn along the path through the trees. Follow the green arrows passing a moss-covered line of stones. When you reach a fork with no signs turn right up some steps to a bench, where you turn left and up some steps. Go past another bench, down some steps and across a footbridge to reach a more open area with silver birch, heading downhill with a sports ground visible down below to your left.

The sports ground is the home of the Border Park Rugby Football Club believed to be the venue of the first ever international football match. According to tradition this was held in 1790 between England and Scotland with the teams made up of the beaters and bearers of the Dukes of Northumberland and Buccleugh. It must have been an extraordinarily violent confrontation as eight players are said to have died in the match with several more dying shortly after as a result of their injuries. God only knows what the referee was doing, if in fact there was one!

3. Cross a footbridge back into the forest and arrive back at the stone bridge to re-trace your steps back across the field and through the gate. Just after the gate, take the right-hand fork to a green area with picnic tables. When you get to a right turn signed **Spur and Arboretum**, take it and follow the blue arrows for the Duke's Trail past a pond and a beautiful large Scots Pine and zig-zag uphill to reach the arboretum. You may wish to spend some time here looking at the trees and visiting the bird hide which has several information panels.

This Scots Pine was planted just after Kielder Castle was built and so is well over 200 years old. The arboretum is on a level open-air platform at the top of the hill and contains a number of trees which are not found in the forest, which is dominated by Sitka Spruce and pines. But the really

Red squirrel near Kielder Castle

striking feature is the beautiful wooden bird and squirrel hide just next to it designed by Ross Associates and built by Forestry Commission staff in July 2010. Inside are some very informative display panels about the birds and other animals which can be found in the area.

4. Follow the Duke's Trail away from the arboretum. When you reach the forest drive, turn right and immediately left into Castle Wood. Keep on the path following the blue arrows ignoring cycle tracks to the left and right and skirt round the car park to a stone wall where you turn right and climb some steps. At the top turn left along a cycleway which you follow for a little and then turn left on the Duke's Trail along a grassy path which eventually drops down through some steps to reach a broad cycle path where you turn left and after about 500m arrive back at the Visitor Centre.

Kielder Castle was built in 1775 as a hunting lodge for the Duke of Northumberland. It is now a Forestry Commission Visitor Centre open between April and the end of September. Along with the school and youth hostel its power comes from a wood-fired community heating scheme in which woodchip produced from forest logs fuels a high efficiency Austrian boiler. It is the first of its kind in England. Since 2010, visitors have been able to savour some real wildlife delights in the Centre. There is live footage of the nesting ospreys which naturally recolonised Northumberland in 2009, having been extinct as a breeding bird in England since about 1840. In 2012, there were in fact two breeding pairs. It is hoped they will return every year after their winter migration to warmer places. In addition, there is an interactive red squirrel exhibition with its own "squirrel-cam". The Visitor Centre also hosts a local history exhibition and an art gallery.

Walk 18: Kielder – Skyspace and Observatory

This walk together with Walk 17 makes a figure of eight walk, with Kielder Castle in the middle. They can be done separately or in one go. This walk follows the River North Tyne for a short distance and then heads into the Forest to visit two very interesting structures – the Skyspace art installation and the Kielder Astronomical Observatory.

Distance	9.3km (5.8 miles)
Difficulty	Moderate
Start	Grid Reference NY632937. Kielder Castle Visitor Centre car park
Parking	The car park is next to Kielder Castle at the northern end of Kielder Water off the C200, the road which goes along the southern edge of the reservoir. In 2012 the parking fee was £4 per day but, once bought, the ticket is valid for all car parks round the reservoir
Maps	OS 1:25000 Explorer OL42, Kielder water & Forest; OS 1:50000 Landranger Sheet 80, Cheviot Hills & Kielder Forest area
Refreshments	The Duke's Pantry tearoom at the Forestry Commission's Kielder Castle Visitor Centre is open all year round. Northumbrian Water has a couple of visitor centres on the reservoir at Tower Knowe and Leaplish but the restaurant opening times are seasonal. There is a youth hostel in Kielder Village. The Angler's Arms in Kielder Village provides accommodation and there are very good pubs at the eastern end of the reservoir which also provide accommodation – the Blackcock Country Inn at Falstone and the Pheasant Inn at Stannersburn

Advice	Kielder Water is notorious for its midges – small irritating flying insects which bite. They appear at the end of May and disappear in September. So, if you are doing the walk at this time, insect repellant is a good idea. Make sure you have plenty of petrol as there are very few petrol stations in the immediate vicinity and, as it is a remote area, petrol is expensive

1. Walk out of the car park and down to the Visitor Centre where you will find a very large finger post with all the trails on it. From the post walk to the right of the Visitor Centre to a sign for the Duchess Trail (green waymarks) and the Minotaur Maze (see Walk 17 for details of this). Drop down some steps through a gap in a fence passing the maze on your right to reach the Kielder Burn where you turn right. Follow the footpath past the footbridge to come out opposite the Angler's Arms where you turn left along the road and over the bridge. Turn left at the junction then immediately right before another road bridge along Lakeside Way. Follow alongside what is now the River North Tyne for just over 500m to Butteryhaugh Bridge and turn right along the road. At the junction with the main road to Kielder, turn right and walk along the verge until you reach a road sign to the left for Kielder Skyspace and Observatory. Turn left up the track to reach a car park and go straight on through a barrier. Carry on uphill and, at a crossroads, go straight on following the signs for Skyspace. Look out for crossbills along the way. When you get to Skyspace, spend some time inside. Also up above it there is a lovely lookout point over the reservoir.

Several members of the finch family can be seen in Kielder Forest at most times of the year including chaffinch, goldfinch, redpoll, greenfinch, bullfinch and siskin. But the most extraordinary member of the family is the crossbill where the tip of the upper part of the bill crosses over the lower part which is perfect for extracting seeds from conifer cones. The birds are usually found high in the trees. The male is easier to spot than the female mainly because of its reddish-orange plumage whereas the female is more greenish. Listen out for the sharp kip-kip-kip call and the sound of falling cones.

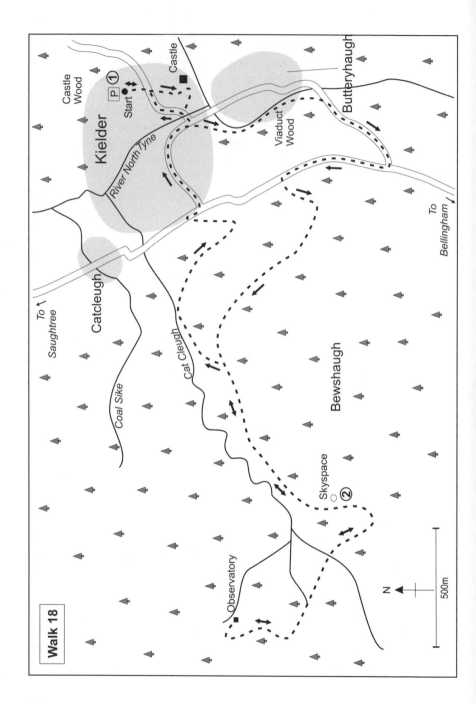

Walk 18

Castle Wood

Kielder

Castle

Start

P 1

Castle

River North Tyne

Butteryhaugh

Viaduct Wood

To Bellingham

Catcleugh

To Saughtree

Coal Sike

Cat Cleugh

Bewshaugh

Skyspace
2

Observatory

N

500m

The Skyspace is one of a number of art installations near Kielder Water. It is an igloo-like structure with a circular hole in the roof which actually makes the sky look solid when viewed from within. It was designed by James Turrell in 2000. Inside, at dawn and dusk, low energy fibre-optic lights switch on, powered by small wind turbines. There is a remarkably tranquil and peaceful atmosphere inside and visitors are known to travel long distances just to sit there and contemplate.

Skyspace

2. After Skyspace, carry on uphill past a barrier, taking in the information panels about the planets, to reach the observatory, where you can access the observation deck and take in the views. Return from the observatory the way you came past Skyspace, ignoring the red mountain bike trail just before it. When you get to the crossroads which you passed on the way up (with a Skyspace sign ¾ mile), walk a little further on and take the footpath to the left into the forest (**return walking route to Kielder Castle**). The path goes gently downhill and reaches a crossroads of paths with wooden barriers on either side of you. Carry straight on here until the path merges with another one which comes from behind you on your left. Again, go straight on to a fork where the right prong has a No Entry sign, so take the left one. Follow the broad path all the way down to the Station Garage and turn right along the road, then left to the village and the castle and back to the car park.

Inside Skyspace

The Kielder Observatory opened in 2008 and takes advantage of the skies above Kielder Water which have very little light pollution. It is a beautifully designed wooden building powered by the sun and the wind. It has two main permanently mounted telescopes and provides a base for the Kielder Observatory Astronomical Society. During the day, you can make use of the viewing deck and take in the magnificent views over Kielder Water and beyond. But the place comes alive at night when there are regular astronomical events. You have to book up for these and you should do so well in advance as they are very popular. A quick look at the Observatory's web-site shows a whole range of interesting night-time events depending upon what is happening in the sky. Public Observing, Family Astronomy, Aurora Night and Comet Night were just a few of the things on offer in late 2012.

Kielder Observatory

Walk 19: Black Middens

The walk heads into Border Reiver Country starting at the village of Lanehead and into the fringes of Kielder Forest. There is an optional extension to visit Black Middens Bastle House, one of the best preserved of such houses. The walk returns over moorland and along the lovely River North Tyne back to the start.

Distance	Full walk: 14.6km (9.7 miles) Shorter walk without extension to Black Middens Bastle House: 12.9km (8.0 miles)
Difficulty	Moderate/Strenuous. It is fairly level but there are some longish rises and some walking over rough ground
Start	Grid Reference NY794858. Layby next to the Village Hall (wooden building) in Lanehead. Lanehead is a mile south of Greenhaugh and can be accessed on minor roads from the B6320 from Otterburn or Bellingham
Parking	There is free parking in the layby
Maps	OS 1:25000 Explorer OL42, Kielder Water and Forest; OS 1:50000 Landranger Sheet 80, Cheviot Hills & Kielder Forest area
Refreshments	The Hollybush Inn in Greenhaugh is a little jewel of a pub. It has accommodation and serves food
Advice	In the summer months, expect flying insects including midges, so come prepared with insect repellant. Some of the paths are indistinct in places and it is easy to lose your way on this walk. Pay close attention to the walk instructions and bring a map and compass just in case. Parts of the walk can get very muddy after wet weather. A walking stick would be useful for some of the long rises and descents

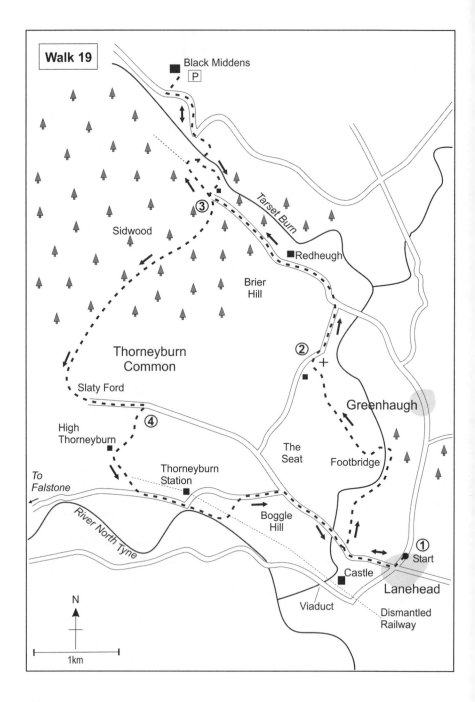

Walk 19

Black Middens
P

Sidwood

Tarset Burn

Redheugh

Brier
Hill

③

Thorneyburn
Common

Slaty Ford

②

+

Greenhaugh

④

High
Thorneyburn

The
Seat

Footbridge

Thorneyburn
Station

To
Falstone

River North Tyne

Boggle
Hill

①
Start

Castle

Lanehead

Viaduct

Dismantled
Railway

N

1km

1. From the layby, walk down the road in a southerly direction and turn right on to a road signed **Donkleywood 3**. Go downhill past a number of cottages to reach a footpath to the right signed **Greenhaugh 1**. Go by the side of a cottage through three wooden gates and straight on across a field, through a gap in a fence to reach a wooden gate in a fence. Turn half left across the field towards the trees to reach a gate leading on to the side of the Tarset Burn. Turn right and follow alongside the burn (do not be tempted by paths straying off to the right) through a number of gates and footbridges to reach a wooded area. Go through the woods passing a kissing-gate to a footbridge over the burn to your left. Cross the bridge and turn left at a farm track to the farm buildings. Go through the farm buildings along a footpath through two metal gates. Head up a rise, and as the path splits by a gnarled tree, keep on the track to the right, pass a waymark and go down a steep drop to cross a stream (take care here as there may be fallen trees around). Work your way up the opposite bank to a large oak tree and go left diagonally across the field to the opposite corner to reach a gate in a stone wall. Turn immediately right, go through a gate then left to follow the fence along the edge of the field. When you reach a stile going back over the fence to your left, turn right away from the fence and head towards the church and house you can see in the distance. There is no clear path but head to the right of a wooden shack near a stone wall before the buildings. Follow the wall right downhill to cross a footbridge and stile, then bear half left up a field towards the house and church. At the top of the bank go through a gate and follow the track along the side of the church.

The parish of Thorneyburn is the largest and most sparsely populated parish in England. St Aidan's Church was built in 1818 by the Greenwich Hospital Commissioners to provide a living for Royal Navy chaplains after the Napoleonic Wars. And as a refreshing 21st Century touch, the current rector (2012) keeps an

St Aidan's Church Thorneyburn

interesting blog which can be found at: www.northumberland rector.blogspot.co.uk/. In the parish nearly 5km to the north of Greenhaugh can be found Highgreen Arts based in an extravagant Scottish baronial manor house built in 1894 for Charles Bell, a Durham mine owner. It is a residential arts centre which runs courses ranging from writing to yoga and every year is home to a different artist in residence. It also houses Bloodaxe Books, the leading independent poetry publisher, whose authors include Tomas Transtromer, winner of the 2011 Nobel Prize for Literature, and Galway Kinnell whose Selected Poems won the Pulitzer Prize in 1982.

2. At the end of the wall go through a gate and turn right along a lane. When you get to a junction turn left towards Redheugh Farm. Just by the farm, there is a permissive footpath on the left to a lovely dovecote (which is over 250 years old) just a short distance across a field. This is well worth a visit. Go back to the road and turn left to enter Kielder Forest and reach the Sidwood Picnic Site where the extension to Black Middens Bastle House begins. If you are not doing this go straight to Paragraph 3. Carry on along the forest track to reach

Redheugh Dovecote

a wooden barrier after about 400m signed **Forestry Vehicles Only**. Go through this to reach a post marked **Black Middens** pointing to the right. Follow this down to the burn and then follow the path to the right and cross a footbridge over the Tarset Burn. Go through a gate at the end of the bridge and follow the field edge turning left alongside a line of trees to emerge on to a sharp bend in a road. Follow the road straight on (in effect turning left) to reach the car park of the Bastle House which you can then visit at your leisure. On your return, after crossing the footbridge, turn left through a kissing-gate and follow a pleasant path along the burn, through another kissing-gate into some trees and then rising back to the picnic site.

A bastle house is a dwelling built so that it can be easily defended. The name comes from the French word *bastille* meaning stronghold. The living quarters were on the first floor with steps leading up to the door and cattle and other livestock were kept underneath. Before the accession of James VI of Scotland to become James I of England in 1603, this border area was turbulent and violent and the bastles were subject to frequent attack. There are several bastle houses in the area and there is, in fact, a Tarset Bastle Trail produced as a partnership between the Forestry Commission and the Tarset Archive Group in 2011, and which you can take from the Sidwood Picnic Site. Black Middens Bastle House is an English Heritage site which is unattended and can be visited at any time. It is one of the better preserved of these houses. Another fine example is Woodhouses Bastle near Holystone (see Walk 13) which has

Black Middens Bastle House

been restored under the guidance of English Heritage and is in a lovely setting next to Holystone Grange.

3. At the picnic site take the bridleway marked **Slaty Ford 1½** taking the right-hand fork after a short distance. Go straight across a broad track crossing your path rising along the bridleway in a south-westerly direction, crossing a gravel track to eventually reach a field corner. Follow the stone wall straight on beside the field and go through a gate. Follow the stone wall initially and then move away from it to the right as the path goes downhill. The path is indistinct and appears and disappears but keep to the right of a deep gully (stay out of this), heading downhill and moving away from the stone wall until you reach a gap in a wall leading on to a track across your path. Turn left to a gate ignoring the bridleway to the right to **Hill House**, cross a ford and continue up the track to a metal gate.

On 20 September 1957, five airmen were killed near Slaty Ford when their Vickers Varsity WL 640 aircraft crashed while on a training flight from the Navigation School at RAF Thorney Island in Sussex. There are some reports of a mining disaster in 1796 at Slaty Ford in which six miners were drowned. But, as always with history, one has to be careful with names and this disaster seems to have happened at Slatyford in Newcastle-upon-Tyne.

4. After about 400m turn right over a stone step stile on to a footpath across a field. Bear half right, and cross a stream to a stile in a wire fence. Turn left over the stile and follow the fence and when you meet another stile back over the fence, turn right across the field and enter a farm. Turn left in front of the house, go through the rightmost of two metal gates, through another gate and then head downhill towards a narrow road. Turn left following a line of ash trees and as the road rises to the left, go straight on over a stile on to a footpath signed **The Hott ½**. Follow this lovely path along the River North Tyne, through a kissing-gate to a suspension bridge. Go on a little further following the embankment as it curves round slightly to the left away from the river. Keep your eyes open for a tunnel under the disused railway ahead of you to your left. It can be difficult to spot but is less than 200m from the bridge, so if you

go further than this, you should backtrack until you find it. Go through this and a gate at the other side and head for a ladder stile over a stone wall on to a road. Follow the road all the way back to Lanehead turning right at the junction you meet on the way. When you get to Lanehead turn left at the junction back to the layby.

The disused railway line is the old Border Counties Railway which went from Hexham through Kielder Forest to Riccarton Junction in Scotland where it met the "Waverley Line". The line was not very economical as the area was so sparsely populated but it stayed open until the late 1950s. One of the stations on the route was Reedsmouth where it met the Wansbeck Valley Railway (the "Wannie Line" – see Walk 21). The station serves the town of Redesmouth (a slightly different

Greystead suspension bridge

spelling) but the railway authorities obstinately refused to change the name of the station until it closed in 1963. The suspension bridge is a fine Grade II listed structure. It is known as the Greystead Bridge or the Hott Chain Bridge and was built in 1862 to allow access to Thorneyburn Station from across the river.

Walk 20: Fonturn Reservoir

This walk is in a lovely quiet area. The full walk skirts the reservoir and then heads off over Greenleighton Moor returning to the reservoir for the homeward leg. The medium and shorter walks concentrate on the lovely fringes of the reservoir itself and miss out Greenleighton Moor.

Distance	Full walk: 12.8km (8.0 miles) Medium walk: 8.3km (5.2 miles) Shorter walk: 5.2km (3.2 miles)
Difficulty	Moderate. Flat nearly all the way. The shorter walk is easy/moderate
Start	Grid Reference NZ 047939. All year car park at Fontburn Reservoir. To get there, take the narrow road signposted to the reservoir off the B6342. When you reach the reservoir, turn right across the dam and then left immediately at the end of the dam. If you turn left when you reach the reservoir instead of right, there is another car park but this is only open in the fishing season
Parking	As above. In 2012, parking was free
Maps	OS 1:25000 Explorer OL42, Kielder Water & Forest; OS 1:50000 Landranger Sheet 81, Alnwick, Morpeth and surrounding area
Refreshments	Few and far between. There is a lovely café at the reservoir called Goats on the Roof which re-opened at the end of March 2013 after being closed for a year. In 2013 it was open Thursdays to Sundays and every day during the school holidays. However it would be wise to check before you go. Otherwise, the Dyke Neuk Inn is in the village of Meldon on the B6343 between Hartburn and Morpeth. It is open all day, serves food and provides accommodation

Advice	Be very wary of the paths marked on the Ordnance Survey map across Greenleighton Moor. They do not bear much relation to the paths on the ground, so stick to the walk instructions for the longer walk which goes across the Moor. Greenleighton Moor can get very boggy so wear suitable footwear

The walk has been vastly improved since 2013 with the introduction of the National Trust's waymarked Greenleighton Walk and Northumbrian Water's waymarked Waterside Trail. These additions have made the walk much easier to follow than in previous years. This walk follows parts of these routes but also includes public footpaths and bridleways and some unmarked walking over Access Land.

The medium and shorter walks are described in paragraphs 1, 4 and 5. The longer walk is an extension described in paragraphs 2 and 3 and rejoins the shorter walks in paragraph 5.

1. Come out of the car park and turn right back across the dam and where the road turns left, go straight ahead through the Fishing Lodge parking area. Follow a footpath alongside a green wire fence away from the car park, dropping down to a track when the fence ends, and continue along this very pleasant waterside path for just over 1 km. The path is well maintained and has wooden walkways, bridges and interesting information panels about the trees to be found here. Ignore the kissing-gate on your left with a green National Trust way mark (**Greenleighton Walk**) and follow the path to the end where you reach a Nature Reserve which you are not allowed to enter, so follow the path up to the left and go through a kissing-gate on to access land. Turn right and follow the fence for a short distance to reach a yellow-topped marker post (the first of many). This is where the shorter and longer walks split. For the shorter walks go to paragraph 4. For the longer walk continue from the next paragraph (2).

Fontburn Reservoir is one of Northumbrian Water's smaller reservoirs and was built by the then Tynemouth Water Company in 1905. There was a

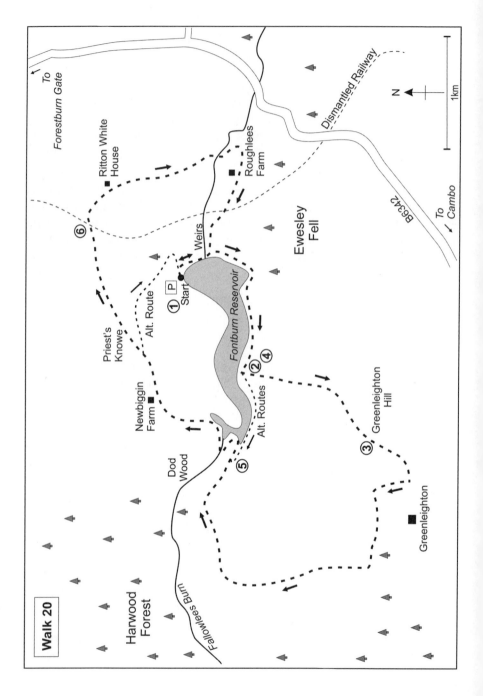

Walk 20

Harwood Forest

Fallowlees Burn

Dod Wood

Newbiggin Farm

Priest's Knowe

Alt. Route

① Start
P

Weirs

Fontburn Reservoir

Alt. Routes

② ④

⑤

Ewesley Fell

Ritton White House

Roughlees Farm

To Forestburn Gate

⑥

Dismantled Railway

B6342

To Cambo

N

1km

Greenleighton Hill

③

Greenleighton

Fontburn Reservoir

large demand for fresh water at this time as the reasons for epidemics of cholera and typhoid were being understood. It now supplies 5½ million gallons of water per day to the Morpeth and Bedlington areas. The eastern side of the reservoir is popular with anglers but the western side is a Nature Reserve. The southern shore is accessible to the public and is fringed by trees – a mixture of conifers and broad-leaved species such as oak, rowan, ash, birch and alder. It is not a particularly good site for bird-watching because of its intense use by anglers during the fishing season. You are likely to see roe deer near the reservoir.

2. For the longer walk turn left at the marker post towards a sheepfold and head straight on in a southerly direction towards the ridge on the horizon, ignoring any paths off to the left and right. As you gradually rise, you will see another large sheepfold ahead of you and another yellow-topped marker post to the right of it but quite a way before it. Head towards this marker post and you will reach a broad grassy track across your path. From the first marker post to this one is just over 800m. You may pass a number of "shake holes" along the way. Turn right along the path

eventually reaching a fence which you follow alongside a quarry and go through two gates with stiles by the side. Follow the path as it sweeps round to the left to the trig point at the top of Greenleighton Hill. Take in the magnificent 360 degree views from here.

Shake holes are dips in the ground formed when the surface is washed down into underground cavities and are often found in limestone areas. Greenleighton Hill is the site of a medieval beacon mentioned during the thirteenth century. The views from the top are tremendous. Limestone has been extracted from Greenleighton Quarry from the early 18th century until 1982. As recently as 1960, a prehistoric stone hammer was found on the edge of the quarry. It can be found at the Great North Museum in Newcastle, formed in 2006 by the merger of the Hancock Museum and Newcastle University's Shefton Museum and Museum of Antiquities.

3. Follow the path past the trig point and when you reach a wire fence, follow it right down a bank and follow the waymarks past a ladder stile on your left (do not cross this stile). Continue straight on alongside a stone wall to reach the corner of a plantation, where you turn right along the edge of the trees. When you reach the next marker post, turn left across a stile into the plantation and follow a needle-strewn path for a short distance. Turn right at a waymark nailed to a tree and after another short distance, turn left alongside a stone wall. Go through a kissing-gate, cross a track and through another kissing-gate. Follow the stone wall to another pair of kissing-gates after which the stone wall gives way to a barbed-wire fence. Continue straight and follow the path round the edge of the plantation, first turning right and then left. At the end of the path, go through a kissing-gate, over a track and across a stile with an **Access Land** sign on to Greenleighton Moor. Turn right and follow the broad path straight across the Moor with the Simonside Ridge virtually directly in front of you in the distance, heading in a northerly direction. There are a number of yellow-topped posts along the way. At the northern edge of the moor the markers will now lead you in an easterly direction back to the reservoir. Follow the path as it passes to the left of a solitary hawthorn tree, to reach a high stone wall with a ladder stile. Cross the stile and follow the path straight on, dropping down and looping slightly round to the right to reach another marker post which you follow towards the

reservoir. When you get to the burn, do not cross it but head straight on towards a gate into the grounds of the reservoir. You now rejoin the shorter walks from Paragraph 5.

The whole of Greenleighton Moor shows evidence of previous occupation. The remains of Iron Age enclosures can be found along the ridge above the Fallowlees Burn and there is a Bronze Age burial mound and cup and ring marked rocks in the area.

4. For the shorter walks, go straight on at the marker post which has both green (National Trust) and yellow (Northumbrian Water Waterside Trail) waymarks and follow the fence along the reservoir. Near the end of the reservoir, cross a stile, passing a large boulder (which has cup marks on it) and head towards a holly tree surrounded by stones. Follow the track round to the right of the tree, cross a stream (where you may find wild orchids in the spring and summer), and continue right following the Waterside Trail alongside the stream to a gate leading back to the reservoir. The longer walk rejoins here.

5. Enter the grounds of the reservoir through the gate. This is an idyllic part of the walk as the path skirts round the reservoir. You are in a Nature Reserve where no fishing is allowed and it is very peaceful and beautiful. Follow the path round the reservoir, crossing a footbridge over the Fallowlees Burn. Continue past the end of the reservoir to another wooden footbridge and on to a fence with two wooden gates. The gate to the right is for the Riverside Trail but, in March 2013, this trail was not complete, so go through the gate straight ahead of you with a bridleway sign on it. Immediately turn right up a bank to a marker post with a waymark for the Waterside Trail pointing to the right towards a hill (the highest point around) with another post on the top. DO NOT FOLLOW THIS. As already mentioned this trail was not complete at the time of writing but when finished, it should make a lovely walk along the north end of the reservoir back to the car park. Instead, at the post, look ahead northwards to a mound and the top of a very tall tree behind it. Head towards this tree. As you get over the mound, you will see Newbiggin Farm ahead of you with the tree to the left of it. Approach the farm, crossing a stile, and you will see that there are actually two magnificent sycamore trees one behind

The Fallowlees Burn

the other. Just in front of the farm, cross a stile and turn right along the farm track, through a metal gate, ignoring the footpath to the left signed **Blueburn Farm 1¼**. When you reach a bridleway sign (**B6342 Coldrife 2**), you have a choice. For the shortest walk, you can follow the farm road all the way back to the car park. Otherwise, turn left at a slight angle off the road on an indistinct path. You will soon see a fenced-off field ahead of you with the road you have just left going alongside one boundary. Head towards the left edge of this fence. At the field corner, follow the fence straight on to reach a metal gate on your right. Go through the gate and turn left, carrying on in the same direction but on the other side of the fence. When the fence turns sharp left, carry straight on downhill, through a wooden gate towards a bridge over a disused railway line.

This railway line is the old Rothbury Line which ran from Rothbury in the north to Scots Gap in the south where it joined the Wansbeck Valley Line (known as the "Wannie Line"). It opened in 1870, but passenger services stopped in 1952 and the line was closed in 1963. The stations along the

way were Longwitton, Ewesley, Fontburn Halt and Brinkburn. Fontburn Halt was used to serve the Whitehouse lime works, colliery and quarries. There are several of these disused railway lines in Northumberland and many of the stations have been converted into private houses.

6. You will see Ritton White House farm up ahead which is where you are heading. On the other side of the bridge, turn left on a broad grassy path to a wooden post (not a marker post) and then on to a proper marker post where you turn right on the bridleway towards the farm. As you approach the farm, go through a metal gate and go towards a couple of metal gates straight ahead in the right hand corner of the farm buildings. Go through the left gate on to a stony track in front of the buildings and turn right over a cattle grid down the farm track. After another cattle grid, as the farm track bears left, go straight on into a very large open field. Head to the left of a group of trees and then down towards the left hand corner to a footbridge over the River Font (this stretch over the field is about 500m). On the other side of the bridge, turn sharp left along the river. The path moves away from the river and loops round back up to Roughlees Farm. Go through a gate to the left of a barn, then through another gate on to the road leading back to the reservoir and the car park.

Roughlees Farm is set up as a rare breed centre (Fontburn Rare Breeds). Their pigs include Oxford Sandy and Black, Tamworth, Berkshire and Middle White. You may also see black Hebridean and Oxford Down sheep together with Buff Orpington and Marsh Daisy chickens.

Walk 21: Hartburn

This walk starts from the quiet village of Hartburn and visits Hartburn Glebe Wood with its amazing bathing grotto. It then goes through woods and across fields to Rothley Castle and back to Hartburn via the village of Middleton. There is a shorter version of the walk which misses out Rothley Castle.

Distance	Full walk: 17.6km (10.9 miles) Shorter walk missing out Rothley Castle: 10.4km (6.5 miles)
Difficulty	Moderate. The longer walk has a short climb to Rothley Castle but it is flat nearly all the way
Start	Grid Reference NZ089861. St Andrew's Church car park in Hartburn on the B6343
Parking	The car park is just by the memorial cross in the village. This is not a public car park. Sometimes it is used for church services (such as weddings) and in this case, park 1km to the north-west on the B6343 (NZ084867) at an unsurfaced layby at a sharp bend in the road and start the walk at Paragraph 2
Maps	OS 1:25000 Explorer OL42, Kielder Water & Forest; OS 1:50000 Landranger Sheet 81, Alnwick, Morpeth and surrounding area
Refreshments	The Dyke Neuk Inn is in the village of Meldon on the B6343 between Hartburn and Morpeth. It is open all day, serves food and provides accommodation. The Ox Inn at Middleton is en-route but does have restricted opening times
Advice	There are three fields in this walk which can cause problems. There are public rights of way across all three but for much of the year, the

Advice (cont'd)	fields are ploughed over and the paths cannot be made out. Sometimes, the paths are clear when the crops are growing but not always. You do have the right to cross the fields but you may wish to consider going round the field boundary, especially if the field is very muddy. Also, some of the fields crossed in this walk have cattle in them

You may like to visit St Andrew's Church before you start the walk proper. In 2012, the church was closed for refurbishment but there are plans for it to re-open when the work has finished. Turn right out of the car park and it is a little way along on the left. The church is a beautiful example of early English work, the tower having been built in about AD1080, soon after the Norman invasion. It has been added to over the centuries. John Hodgson, the famous historian of Northumberland, was vicar here from 1833 until his death in 1845 and is buried in the churchyard. Inside, near the door, is a large wooden chest called Cromwell's Money-Box which was used by Oliver Cromwell to carry bullion. Also near the door are two stone coffins which were ploughed up in fields nearby.

*Cromwell's money box in
St Andrew's Church*

1. Turn left at the car park and walk along the road past the memorial cross. Pass the houses and you will see a deep gorge down to your right. Just before a sharp left-hand bend, take the footpath to the right into Hartburn Glebe Wood. Do not go over the stone bridge ahead but drop down to the right and down some steps to the Hart

Burn. Cross a little wooden bridge and follow the path along the burn past an idyllic little spot with cliffs on the other side. As the burn curves round to the left, you will come across the bathing grotto. You will want to spend some time looking round here. After the grotto, follow the path along the burn rising up into the woods, taking care with the steep drop to your right. At the fork in the path, go straight on along the top rather than dropping down to the right. Come out on to the main road again and turn right. Follow the road, taking care with the traffic, until you come to a sharp left-hand bend with a parking space to the right. This is the alternative starting point to the walk.

Hartburn Glebe grotto

Hartburn Glebe Wood is managed by the Woodland Trust and is a little gem. It is on the steep sides of the Hart Burn where badgers, otters and red squirrels can be found. In the spring, bluebells abound and for much of the year, the smell of wild garlic permeates the air. The really striking feature of the wood is the bathing grotto, a Grade II listed natural cave which has been fashioned into a beautiful chapel-like structure. It is linked to the burn by a low tunnel to preserve the modesty of bathers! It was built by the Reverend Doctor John Sharpe, an 18th century vicar of Hartburn. There is a deep pool at a bend in the Burn called the Baker's Chest where Viking raiders are said to have hidden their booty. The Devil's Causeway, an old Roman route, also crosses the site. It really is an unusual, magical place.

2. Leave the road and take the bridleway (**Longwitton Dene 1½**). Follow the path to the burn and cross the footbridge, ignoring the bridleway to the right to **Wittonstone and South Witton** and go straight along the footpath to **Longwitton Dene**. Pass the Garden

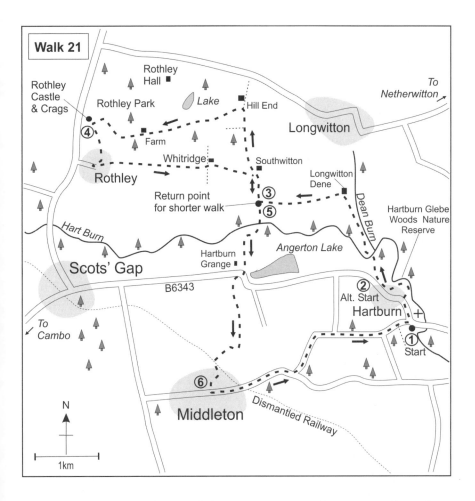

House on your left which has its own resident peacock and go through a wooden gate. When you reach a large open field ahead, follow the path alongside it through the woods. Go through a gate, across a field to another gate just in front of some farm buildings. Go through the left hand side of the buildings with a large corrugated iron barn on your left to turn left on to a bridleway through some fields. As you approach some trees, the path splits. Take the less obvious path through a gap in the hedge and immediately turn right along the bridleway with the hedge now on your right. At the end of the field, enter another field and carry on along the boundary. As you approach Southwitton Farm away to your right, head towards a wooden fence with a gate and some public bridleway signs on it. If you are doing the shorter walk, you should turn left across the field following the instructions from paragraph 5 onwards.

3. For the longer walk go through the gate and head towards the farm along the edge of a field and go left round the house to a large field ahead. There is a bridleway straight across this field which is sometimes ploughed over and invisible, so go straight across heading toward the right hand corner of a wood on the other side. Go across a wooden bridge and head straight on with a stone wall on your left. At the end of the wall go through a gate to reach a metalled lane which you follow straight on for about 250m up a rise towards Hill End Farm. Just before the farm turn left through a metal gate on to a footpath signed **Rothley 1¾**. Head diagonally across the field towards the bottom left hand corner (about 750m). Go through a wooden gate into the woods, follow the path through

Rothley Castle

the trees to reach a metal gate in a stone wall. Go through the gate and turn left across a field and over a pair of stiles into another field. Go straight on to reach a metal gate, then another and head towards a house. Cross a ladder stile over a stone wall and head towards the left hand corner of the garden of the house, crossing a footbridge along the way. Follow the fence round the house to reach a wooden gate, then turn left along a track. As the track turns sharp right, ignore the metal gate leading straight on off the road but go through the metal gate on the track and then immediately through the metal gate on your left into a field, and follow the path uphill to Rothley Castle.

Rothley Castle is a ruined folly on the National Trust's Wallington Estate. It has a dramatic setting at the top of Rothley Crags with magnificent 360 degree views. It is a Grade II listed building built by Sir Walter Blackett of Wallington in 1755. It is an imitation stronghold built to resemble a medieval castle with arrow slits and pointed windows and doors. The centrepiece of the Wallington Estate is the nearby Wallington Hall, a National Trust property, dating from 1688 and home to the Blackett and Trevelyan families. It is a very popular place to visit and, among many other things, has a fascinating collection of dolls houses.

4. From Rothley Castle, do not go back the way you came but turn left downhill in a southerly direction towards a stone wall, go through a red metal gate, then straight across a short stretch to another red metal gate. Follow the path alongside a wire fence and as the fence ends, continue right along the path and then left at a stone wall, through a wooden gate to emerge onto a track by some farm buildings. Immediately turn left along the bridleway (**Whitridge 1, Longwitton Dene House**). Follow the bridleway all the way to Whitridge passing through 2 large double metal gates and a wooden gate. When you reach a track crossing your path turn left up to Whitridge, then right (**Southwitton ½, Hartburn Grange 1½**). When you get to Southwitton, retrace your steps round the buildings, and turn right down the field back to the wooden gate at the bottom.

5. Follow the bridleway straight across the field. This is the second problematic field and you may find you cannot make out the path. You can go right then left and left again round the field boundary

or you can go straight across. Whichever you choose you should reach a wooden gate on the other side with a bridleway sign into a wood. After a very short distance the path splits and you take the right hand fork going downhill and across a footbridge over the Hart Burn. Go straight on up a rise following the bridleway as it turns right and enter a field through a metal gate. Turn left across the field veering slightly away from the wall. There is no clear path but as you go across you will see a house ahead of you and you should head to the left of this. Eventually you meet a track which you follow to the field corner, then through a metal gate on to the B6343. Turn right, and just opposite Hartburn Grange, turn left through a gate on to a public footpath (**Middleton 1**). Follow this distinctly underused and faint path as it gradually goes downhill. As you approach the bottom, keep your eyes open for a stile into a field on your left. Enter the field and go straight across bearing slightly to your right. As you get to the top of a rise, head towards a stile, then a ladder stile to the right of a solitary tree. Cross the stiles and follow the path along the edge of a field with the fence on your left. At the end of the field cross a steep ditch on to a ladder stile, then turn half right to a stile on the other side of the field corner. Cross the stile into the third problematic field. Again there is supposed to be a path straight across but much of the time it is just not there. You can follow the field boundary by turning right then left then left again. There are gates on the way but you should pass these to get to a stile. Cross the stile over a disused railway line then over another stile into a field. Go across the field heading just to the left of a copse of trees.

The disused railway line is that of the Wansbeck Valley Railway, known as "the Wannie Line" which ran from Morpeth to Reedsmouth where it connected with the Border Counties Railway. The Wannie Line met the Rothbury Branch Line (mentioned in Walk 20) at Scots Gap. The line opened in 1862, with passenger services ending in 1952 and the last goods train running in 1966. There is a north-east expression "in the wilds of wannie", meaning far away, out in the wilderness. This relates to the area traversed by the Wannie Line which passed just to the north of Great Wanney Crag. The border area had a violent past and the expression "beyond the hills of Wannie" had the added meaning of being an area populated by utterly lawless people, so not a wise place to venture.

6. Go through a gate, down a steepish bank, over a stile on to a footbridge over a stream. Turn left and follow a path alongside a stone wall towards a road. Turn left on the road through Middleton past the Ox Inn (where you may want to stop for refreshments). Keep on this road for another 3.3km all the way back to Hartburn.

Walk 22: Mitford

This walk is from the village of Mitford near Morpeth. The paths are well maintained thanks to the Morpeth Walking Festival. The walk has a very pleasant stretch along the River Wansbeck and passes by the ruins of Mitford Castle.

Distance	11.4km (7.1 miles)
Difficulty	Moderate. Flat nearly all the way
Start	Grid Reference NZ172860. Mitford on the B6343
Parking	On the roadside in Mitford
Maps	OS 1:25000 Explorer 325, Morpeth & Blyth; OS 1:50000 Landranger Sheet 81, Alnwick, Morpeth and surrounding area
Refreshments	The Plough Inn in Mitford serves food and real ale. It is closed between 3.00 and 6.00 pm on weekdays but is open all day from 12.00 at the weekend. The Dyke Neuk Inn is in the village of Meldon further along the B6343. It is open all day, serves food and provides accommodation
Advice	The walk goes along the B6343 for some of the time. This is narrow in places and traffic travels quite fast along it. There is no pavement so you have to walk along the verge. Take care

The village of Mitford is at the meeting of the Rivers Font and Wansbeck and has been the home of the Mitford family since before the Norman Conquest, although they do not live there now. Many of the Mitford family were talented writers. These include Mary Russell Mitford (1787-1855, author of *Our Village*), William Mitford (1744-1827, author of *The History of Greece*), Philip Meadows Taylor (1808-1876, author of the best-selling *Confessions of a Thug* about the Thugee cult in India) and Jack Mitford (1782-1831, a naval officer who wrote *Johnny Newcombe in the*

Navy among other things and who turned to drink and semi-vagrancy in his later life). But the most celebrated Mitfords were the six Mitford sisters all born in the early part of the 20th Century. The eldest and probably best-known was Nancy Mitford, a talented novelist and biographer, but her five sisters provided a colourful mixture of extremes and eccentricity. Two of them were fascist sympathisers. Diana, the third sister, was married to Sir Oswald Moseley, leader of the British Union of Fascists. The fourth sister, Unity Valkyrie Mitford, conceived in the town of Swastika, Ontario (absolutely true!) was a renowned admirer of Adolf Hitler. In complete contrast, the fifth sister, Jessica was a free-thinker, author and communist who married an American civil rights lawyer in 1943 after her first husband was killed in World War II. Pamela, the second sister, was an animal lover and introduced the Appenzeller Spitzhauben breed of chicken from Switzerland. The youngest and last surviving sister, Deborah, was born in 1920 and is the Dowager Duchess of Devonshire. She has written several books, many of them about Chatsworth House.

Outside the Old Post Office in Mitford, now a private house, is a defunct stone fountain on the site of an old well. According to legend a miracle occurred here when a monk used the water to restore sight to the blind and to cure dysentery.

The old well at Mitford

1. Head down towards the river past the Plough Inn. Cross the road bridge and take the footpath left on the east side of the River Font (**West Benridge 1, Newton Park 1¼**). Go down a few steps and walk alongside the river, ignoring a footpath going steeply uphill to your right, to reach a gate into a field. Cross the field on to a track leading up to your right towards a house, where you go through a gate into a small farmyard. Go through two more gates past the

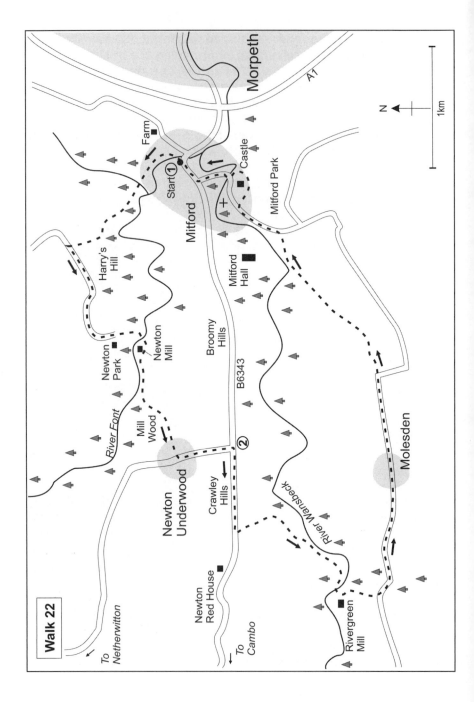

Walk 22

Morpeth

A1

N

1km

Farm

Start ①

Castle

Mitford Park

Mitford

Harry's Hill

Mitford Hall

Newton Park

Newton Mill

Broomy Hills

River Font

Mill Wood

B6343

②

Newton Underwood

Crawley Hills

Molesden

River Wansbeck

To Netherwitton

Newton Red House

To Cambo

Rivergreen Mill

farm building and head downhill and across a stone bridge over Mitford Dene, after which you go through a gate on to a tractor track (often very muddy). Follow the track or the drier path on the bank alongside it up through the woods and go through a gate at the top into an open field where you carry straight on along the right-hand boundary. At the top of the field, turn left and follow this boundary along a barbed wire fence to the field edge where you go through a gate or across a ladder stile turning right along the tree-lined bridleway between two fields. The path reaches a very narrow road where you turn left and follow the road for 850m to reach Newton Park, ignoring any paths to the right. Bear left round the farmhouse, pass some barns on your right and go southwards along the track. As you approach the river, keep your eyes peeled for a footbridge to your right, just before the track sweeps to the right. Cross the bridge and walk across a field heading to the left of the house at Newton Mill. Just before the house go through a gate on your left and on to another gate, the path being just on the edge of the property. Go across a small field, then through a gate next to a stile into Mill Wood. Follow the path through the wood for 400m and just before the end of the wood, a narrow path goes off to the left for a very short distance into a field where you take the footpath half right across the field towards a farmhouse. **This narrow path is easy to miss so if you come out of the end of the wood on to open ground, you have gone too far and need to go back.** On your way to the farmhouse, cross a stile into another field and head towards the left of the house. Go through a gate and follow a track between two houses to reach a narrow road where you turn left. Continue for 450m to the B6343.

The walks in this area near Morpeth are very well maintained, with good footpaths and signs. This is mainly due to the Morpeth Annual Walking Festival, a fantastic event for all ages and abilities. It happens in September or October each year and is managed and delivered by the Greater Morpeth Development Trust, a community led organisation. Long may it continue.

2. Turn right and follow the road for about 700m, taking care as the road can be busy and the verge is narrow. As you approach a set of buildings and a double-bend sign, take the unsigned track to the left towards Rivergreen Mill. This is a lovely stretch of 1.25km as

the track drops down, then bends right to reach the River Wansbeck which you follow close alongside to reach a footbridge across the river. Go past Rivergreen Mill, but **do not** go straight on towards a house. Instead, cross a stretch of grass in front of the mill, and turn left up a very narrow road, climbing uphill to reach a junction. Turn left at the junction to reach the hamlet of Molesden after 1.25km, then after a further 600m, when the road turns sharp right, go straight on off the road through a metal gate on a public footpath into a field (**Mitford Park 1 mile**). Go along the field edge and at the end of the field, cross a stile and a footbridge, and follow the field edge, at first left and then right. Follow the yellow footpath signs across a number of fields, eventually passing Mitford Hall which you can see on your left. At the end of the last field, go through a kissing-gate on to a minor road and turn left. Follow the road for about 300m and turn right over a stile along a public footpath (**Mitford Steads ½**) with the ruined Mitford Castle in front of you. Follow the path along the right-hand side of the Castle. The path on the ground does not follow the path on the Ordnance Survey map. As you pass the Castle, you can go up the

Mitford Castle

mound to explore it, and return to the path. Follow the path as it sweeps left round the base of the mound and head towards the corner of the field where it meets a stream and the trees on your right come to an end. Cross a stile next to a bridge over the stream and turn left following the river to some stone steps on to the road where you turn right to reach the B6343. Turn right at the junction and return to Mitford.

Mitford Castle is a Grade I listed building and was built in the first half of the 12th Century by William Bertram, the founder of Brinkburn Priory. He was the son of Sir Richard Bertram, one of William the Conqueror's knights, and Sybilla de Mitford. The castle had a short and turbulent history, having been seized by King John in 1215 and finally captured and dismantled by Alexander III of Scotland in 1318. The castle is unusually shaped and has the only five-sided keep in England (the remains of which you see today). Since 1993, the Mitford Estate, including Mitford Hall and Mitford Castle has been in the hands of the Shepherd family who own Shepherd Offshore.

Walk 23: Colt Crag and Hallington Reservoirs

This walk skirts the sides of two lovely reservoirs near the A68 north of Hexham. It also visits two churches, one of which is at Thockrington, which has a dramatic setting and is where William Beveridge is buried.

Distance	16.8 km (10.4 miles)
Difficulty	Moderate/strenuous. It is a longish walk but there are no hills to climb although there are some short stretches over rough ground
Start	Grid Reference NY954754. Colwell village
Parking	There is free parking on the roadside in Colwell
Maps	OS 1:25000 Explorer OL43, Hadrian's Wall, Haltwhistle & Hexham; OS 1:50000 Landranger Sheet 87, Hexham & Haltwhistle
Refreshments	The Errington Arms on the A68/B6318 roundabout has accommodation and food. The Barrasford Arms in nearby Barrasford has accommodation and is renowned for its food
Advice	Some of the fields crossed in this walk have cattle in them. The walk crosses the A68 in two places. This is a busy road with fast-moving traffic so take care when crossing

1. From the B6342 in Colwell, take the minor road signposted **West Woodburn 9 miles**. Follow this road for just over 1km to reach the A68. Go straight over the A68 (take care) to a road signposted **Great Swinburne ½ mile**. Follow this road round the field on your right, bending sharply right to reach St Mary's Catholic Church. At the fork at the church go straight on. Go past Mill Cottage on your left. Leave the road through a gate and go straight along a track with

an abandoned 18th century tithe barn on your left with red doors and shutters.

St Mary's Church is a small chapel with a lovely cross in the churchyard dated 1858 and a rather splendid topiary hedge along the side. In the east of Great Swinburne are the remains of a deserted medieval village, destroyed by the Scots in 1320. Near to Great Swinburne is the site of Swinburne Castle. The Castle has long since disappeared and in 1760 a mansion was built out of the ruins by Thomas Riddell. In 2000, a new country house was built on the site which incorporated a 16th century wing and an 18th century orangery. It is a private residence. Within the grounds is the striking Swinburne Standing stone. Eleven feet in height and spreading out at the top like a human hand, it is the largest prehistoric monolith in Northumberland. The stone has

The tithe barn near Great Swinburne

cup-marks carved on both sides and is assumed to date from the Bronze Age (2500 to 800 BC). Unfortunately, you cannot view this as it is on private land.

2. Follow the track over the Swin Burn, then about 50m further on go through a gate to your left. Follow the path for almost 1km through hedgerows, crossing a metalled road after about ½km with gates on either side. At the end of the path you come out on to a sharp bend of a metalled road, where you turn left. Follow the road for nearly 900m to reach Barrasford Park on your left. Just opposite the park entrance is a gate leading to a public bridleway signposted **A68 ½ mile**. The path goes sharp right (almost going back on

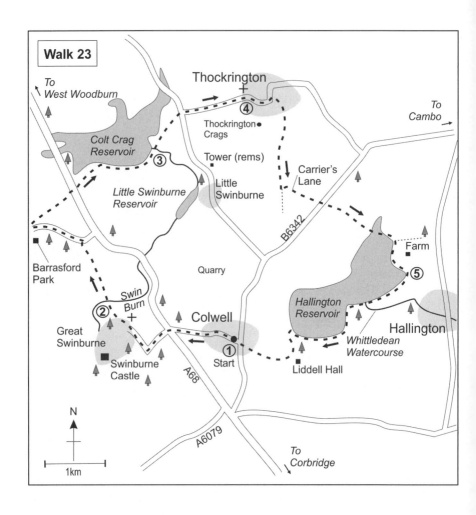

Walk 23

To West Woodburn

Colt Crag Reservoir

③

Little Swinburne Reservoir

Thockrington

④

Thockrington Crags

Tower (rems)

Little Swinburne

To Cambo

Carrier's Lane

B6342

Quarry

Hallington Reservoir

Farm

⑤

Barrasford Park

Swin Burn

②

Great Swinburne

Colwell

①

Start

Liddell Hall

Whittledean Watercourse

Hallington

Swinburne Castle

A68

N

A6079

To Corbridge

1km

yourself) and becomes rather indistinct, but head slightly to the right of some raised ground in the middle of the field and you will soon see a gate and a ladder stile on to the A68. Cross the A68 (take care) and go through a gate on to a public bridleway across Folly Moss. Do not take the obvious track that follows the boundary wall but head half left across the Moss. Go through a gate at the corner of a stone wall into the grounds of Colt Crag Reservoir. Go straight on and follow the path around the reservoir to cross the dam.

Colt Crag Reservoir is owned by Northumbrian Water. It was built in 1884 for the Newcastle and Gateshead Water Company. Much of it is surrounded by Scots pine and Norway spruce, but birch and beech trees are also present. In the summer months, the beautiful great-crested grebe can be seen as they return here to breed. Red squirrels can still be found here and badgers are known to use the site. Both pipistrelle and noctule bats feed around the north-eastern end of the reservoir.

3. After the dam, go straight ahead through a gate across a field and through another gate. Do not follow the path straight on but at a small wall (about 8m long) with a wooden fence turn left. You will soon see on your right a road sign on the other side of the field. Head off in the direction of the sign across rough ground. There are paths round here but they appear and disappear. Go through a gate on to a junction of a narrow metalled road. Go straight across and take the road signposted **Thockrington 1 mile**. This is a gated road and you will soon see a church ahead of you and there are sweeping views of the Tyne Valley to your right. You may wish to visit St Aidan's Church when you reach Thockrington.

St Aidan's Church in Thockrington is built on a spur of the Whin Sill and affords a marvellous view of South Northumberland. It is an ancient church and was first built in AD1100 by the Umfraville family. On the floor are two carved grave covers, one of a 14th century woman in a kerchief, wimple and kirtle. William Beveridge, whose famous report was used as the basis of the Welfare State, is buried in the graveyard with his wife Janet. There was once a village to the north of the church but this was wiped out in 1847 when a sailor returned home bringing cholera with him.

4. After the church you approach a farm. There are two signs before the farm. Take the public bridleway **Colwell 1¼ miles**, not the public footpath. Follow the bridleway for about 1½km across fields and alongside a wall, passing through gates between the fields. You will eventually reach a broad track across your path – this is Carrier's Lane. Turn left along Carrier's Lane, go through a gate and across a big field with cattle and sheep. The cattle can be a bit frisky here. After about 600m go through a gate, cross the B6342, and through another gate (**Byway** signs). After about 1km you come to a wood. Go straight on through a gate and over the Hallington Reservoir. On the other side of the reservoir go through a gate on your right

St Aidan's Church at Thockrington

on to a broad grassy track along the side of the reservoir. Follow the path for just over 600m to reach a gate near Cheviot Farm (which is private).

The ordnance survey map shows a 'Tumulus' a little to the south-east of Cheviot Farm. It is believed to be a Bronze Age burial mound. Also to the north of the farm are a number of cairns and one or more of these may have been used as prehistoric burial mounds.

5. Turn right and follow the reservoir round for over 1km until you reach a car park and some buildings. Do not take the road over the reservoir but turn left through a gate and follow the track round the reservoir for a further 1¼km crossing a metal bridge. You eventually reach a corner of the reservoir with a wooden shelter with a seat inside it. The main path carries on to the right following

the reservoir but you should turn left through the trees away from the water. Go through a metal gate in a stone wall, through the wood to another metal gate into a field. Follow the path across the field to come out near Liddell Hall. Do not take the path to the Hall but go straight on for about 700m back to Colwell.

Hallington Reservoir is made up of two small reservoirs, Hallington East and Hallington West, separated by a dam across which you can drive to a car park. They are part of a series of reservoirs from the Scottish Border to near Newcastle, which are connected by aqueducts and tunnels. A very rare plant, the small-fruited yellow sedge, can be found near the dam between the reservoirs. The reservoir is a wintering ground for many wildfowl, and native white-clawed crayfish are found within the aqueduct

Hallington Reservoir

Walk 24: Seaton Sluice

This is a varied walk from Seaton Sluice just over the border into Northumberland from Tyne & Wear. It visits the picturesque Holywell Dene and Holywell Pond and then moves on for an optional visit to Seaton Delaval Hall, returning on a fine beach walk to Seaton Sluice. The walk can be made considerably shorter by returning to the start from Seaton Delaval Hall.

Distance	Full walk 15.4km (9.6 miles) Shorter walk 9.2km (5.7 miles)
Difficulty	Moderate. Flat nearly all the way
Start	Grid Reference NZ332771. Car park off the roundabout on the A193 just north of the harbour at Seaton Sluice after the road bridge
Parking	As above. In 2012, parking was free. There are toilets and baby-changing facilities
Maps	OS 1:25000 Explorer 316, Newcastle upon Tyne; OS 1:50000 Landranger Sheet 88, Newcastle upon Tyne
Refreshments	There are plenty of places to eat and drink in Seaton Sluice
Advice	This walk can be done at any time but, if doing the full walk, is perhaps best when the tide is out to take full advantage of the beach section at the end. Autumn is also a good time to do it as there are plenty of blackthorn bushes (for picking sloes) near the B1325 car park and Holywell Dene is famous locally for blackberries (but get there early in the season as a lot of people know about them!!). Seaton Delaval Hall is worth a visit. It is a National Trust property but is not open all year or every day. Also the Church of Our Lady is only open at very

Advice (cont'd)	restricted times between May and September. So it is best to check both of these beforehand if you wish to visit. If you are interested in bird-watching, November to March are the best times for Holywell Pond due to the large numbers of winter visitors

1. From the car park, go back to the roundabout, turn left along the road and cross over before the bridge. At the bridge, take the footpath to the right down some steps and follow the path into Holywell Dene. As the dene bears left, and you can see a large pipe crossing high above it, you will find a bench and just to the right of this at the top of a bank you will see a ruin with a steep path leading up to it. This is the Starlight Castle, and you may want to make a short detour to see the little that remains of it.

The story of Starlight Castle is an unusual one. It was built in 1750 as a result of a bet between Sir Francis Delaval and an actor friend, Samuel

The remains of Starlight Castle

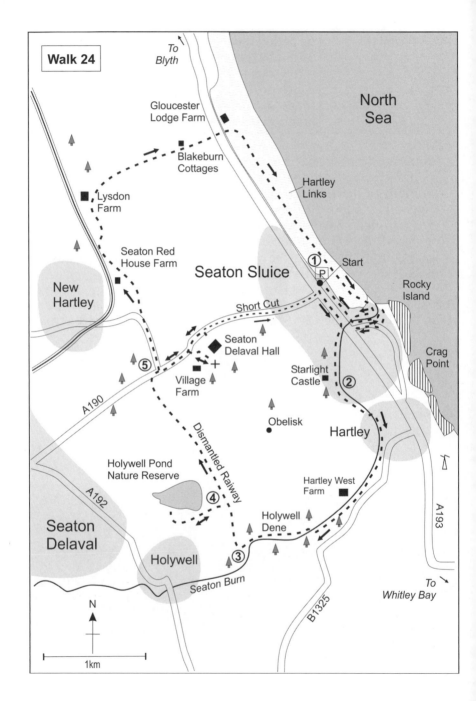

Walk 24

To Blyth

North Sea

Gloucester Lodge Farm

Blakeburn Cottages

Hartley Links

Lysdon Farm

Seaton Red House Farm

Seaton Sluice

New Hartley

① Start

P

Rocky Island

Short Cut

Seaton Delaval Hall

Starlight Castle

②

Crag Point

⑤

A190

Village Farm

Obelisk

Hartley

Dismantled Railway

Holywell Pond Nature Reserve

④

A192

Hartley West Farm

A193

Seaton Delaval

Holywell

Holywell Dene

③

Seaton Burn

To Whitley Bay

B1325

N

1km

Foote, who was famous for his satirical sketches. Francis accepted a bet from Foote that he could not build a castle in a day. Using prepared stone, a team of builders is said to have built the castle in 24 hours by starting when the stars were shining and finishing by daylight. It is now a complete ruin but it was occupied in the 19th century.

2. Return to the path, continue underneath the pipe, cross a footbridge over the burn and turn right. The path wends its way along the other side of the burn to eventually reach a parking area by the B1325. Do not enter the car park, but take the path to the right, then immediately where the path splits take the right fork and follow the path to the edge of the burn and then along to a bridge. Cross a stile and go straight across the lane into the woods along a footpath (with a green sign). Continue along the wooded south bank of the burn and cross over a wooden footbridge, turning left on the other side. Join another track, go through a squeeze stile and follow the north side of the burn until it eventually goes through a tunnel. Just before the tunnel, follow the path up a bank to a squeeze stile leading on to an old waggonway. There are some interesting information panels here.

North Tyneside has several miles of waggonways which are part of its coal mining heritage. Horses pulled coal at first along wooden rails which were later replaced by iron ones. This practice continued until the arrival of the locomotive in the first half of the 19th century. George Stephenson used the Killingworth Waggonway for early trials with his locomotive which led to the standard gauge for railways: 4 feet 8½ inches between the inside edges of the rails. About 60% of the world's railways use this gauge.

3. Follow the waggonway to the right under a bridge. After about 400m, you reach a marker post pointing left to Holywell Pond through a kissing-gate and up some steps. If you are interested in water birds, it is only a short detour. You soon reach a bird hide and if you follow the edge of the field past the hide, you come to a gate at the top end. Through the gate, you enter a Nature Reserve belonging to the Northumberland Wildlife Trust and there is an information panel here. You can follow a path to another bird hide for which you need a key from the Wildlife Trust, but you can still watch the birds from outside the hide.

Holywell Pond is a nature reserve managed by Northumberland Wildlife Trust. In addition to the more permanent birds, it attracts many migrating birds as it is close to the sea. Wigeon, goldeneye, mallards and tufted ducks are commonly seen especially between November and March. Herons are also often found. Little and great crested grebes, pochard and graylag geese are known to breed here.

4. Return to the waggonway and continue left for about 1¼km to reach the A190. Turn right and you will see a road to the left signed **New Hartley ¾**. If you are doing the longer walk, we shall return here after visiting Seaton Delaval Hall and the Church of Our Lady, unless you don't want to visit them in which case, go to the next paragraph. If you are doing the shorter walk, this also passes Seaton Delaval Hall. Continue along the pavement on the A190 until you reach a sharp bend to the left. The Church of our Lady is along a track to your right. After visiting the church return to the main road and turn right to reach the entrance to Seaton Delaval Hall, which you can visit if you wish. If you are doing the shorter walk, carry on past the Hall along the A190 all the way back to Seaton Sluice. The road comes out at the roundabout near the car park. If you are doing the longer walk, retrace your steps back along the A190 to the turn-off to New Hartley.

Seaton Delaval Hall is now in the care of the National Trust and opened to visitors in 2010. It was designed by John Vanburgh, the architect of Blenheim Palace and Castle Howard, and is regarded as one of the most important houses in England. The main house was virtually destroyed by fire in 1822 and is now pretty much an empty but magnificent shell, but the east and west wings survived. It has formal gardens with colourful borders and is home to a magnificent weeping ash tree. But alongside the fabulous building is the equally interesting story of the notorious Delaval family who inhabited the Hall for more than 700 years. Many of the family were level-headed and respectable and included MPs, admirals and engineers, but there was also a frivolous, pleasure-seeking group of individuals, epitomised by the "Gay Delavals" who were around in the 18th Century. Foremost among these was Sir Francis Blake Delaval, a practical joker, gambler and adulterer of the first order. He was famous for hosting extravagant, wild parties at the Hall. His married niece, Sarah, had public affairs with the Duke of York and Lord Strathmore and her brother John died at the age of 20 after being kicked in the crotch by a laundry

Seaton Delaval Hall

maid whom he was molesting! In 1717, the Delavals inherited Ford Castle (see Walk 1) and so started the Curse of the Delavals when according to legend, the ram's head above the main entrance to the Castle declared that no male Delaval would die in his bed while the family held both Ford and Seaton estates. This is exactly what happened to Francis' brothers: two died in battle, one was drowned, one was killed in the Lisbon earthquake of 1755, one died at the breakfast table, another fell off his horse and Francis himself collapsed and died after a huge meal at the age of 44. The curse lapsed when Ford Castle became the property of the Marquis of Waterford (see Walk 1).

For a full account of the history of the Delavals, Martin Green, a local author, has written an excellent book, *The Delavals a Family History* which can be purchased at Seaton Delaval Hall.

5. Turn off the A190 to New Hartley until you reach a sharp left turn. Go straight on to a bridleway and follow a lane to Seaton Red House Farm. Follow the path through the farm buildings, past the front of some houses to reach Lysdon Farm and turn right along a clear path towards the sea. Follow the path for about 1¼km to reach a metal gate on to the main A193 road. Cross straight over on to a path leading to the dunes. You cross a cycle path, which you can

follow back to the car park if you wish, but we shall be going through the dunes on to the beach. Turn right along the beach for about 2km. When you get to the harbour, work your way right along the channel to the road bridge crossing the water. If you want to visit the harbour area, there are a couple of good pubs and an interesting display board outside the Kings Arms about the history of the village. To get there, cross the footbridge which is under the road bridge. When you have finished in the harbour area, go back over the road bridge to the car park.

Seaton Sluice gets its name from the sluice gate built by Ralph Delaval in the late 17th century to prevent the harbour from silting up. In 1764, Sir John Delaval improved the harbour by cutting a new channel eastwards to the sea through solid rock to create a new entrance and dock. From that point on, Seaton Sluice became a thriving port used for the export of coal (carried along the waggonways) and bottles. The bottles were made at the Royal Hartley Bottleworks which was founded by Thomas Delaval in 1763. The interesting octagonal shaped building next to the Waterford Arms on the edge of the harbour was built in the early 18th century as the Harbour Master's Office and was later used as a reading room for workers from the bottleworks.

Seaton Sluice

Walk 25: Hadrian's Wall

This is a classic and popular walk along one of the best preserved and dramatic stretches of Hadrian's Wall. The walk includes an optional visit to Housesteads Fort, the best preserved fort on the Wall, which is passed on the way.

Distance	12.2km (7.6 miles)
Difficulty	Moderate/Strenuous. There are several ups and downs along the undulating wall, some of which are quite steep. The return leg can get pretty boggy
Start	Grid Reference NY951677. Steel Rigg pay and display car park which can be accessed along a minor road from the B6318. It is sign-posted. The turn-off is about 4.5km west of the car park for Housesteads Fort
Parking	As above. In 2012, parking was £3 per day (cash and credit card accepted, motor bikes and cycles free) and the ticket can be used at five other nearby sites on the same day: Walltown, Cowfields, Once Brewed, Housesteads and Broccolita
Maps	OS 1:25000 Explorer OL43, Hadrians' Wall, Haltwhistle & Hexham; OS 1:50000 Landranger Sheet 87, Hexham & Haltwhistle
Refreshments	The Twice Brewed Inn is on the B6318, a little to the west of the turn-off to Steel Rigg. It serves food and drink all day and provides accommodation
Advice	The return stretch along the base of the wall can get pretty muddy. There are cattle along the way which appear quite used to people

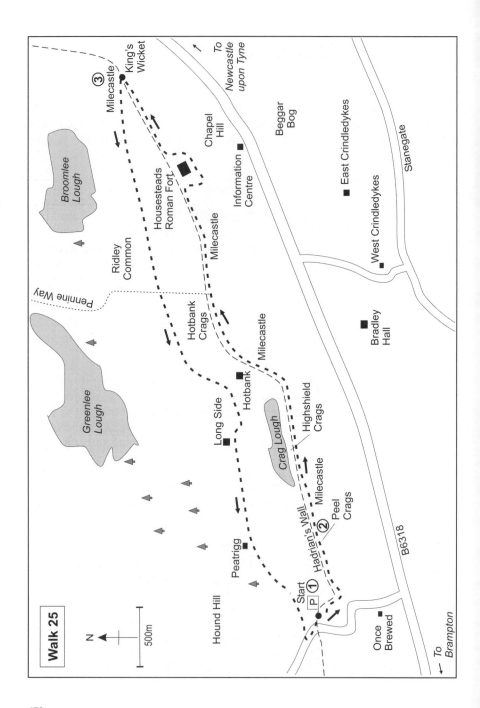

Walk 25

N

500m

Broomlee Lough

Greenlee Lough

Crag Lough

Hound Hill

Peatrigg

Long Side

Hotbank

Highshield Crags

Peel Crags

Once Brewed

To Brampton

B6318

Start

P ①

Hadrian's Wall

Milecastle

②

Milecastle

Hotbank Crags

Pennine Way

Ridley Common

Housesteads Roman Fort

Milecastle

Chapel Hill

Milecastle

Information Centre

Beggar Bog

East Crindledykes

West Crindledykes

Stanegate

Bradley Hall

Milecastle

③

King's Wicket

To Newcastle upon Tyne

172

Hadrian's Wall

Hadrian's Wall is a World Heritage Site and stretches for 73 miles across the north of England from Bowness-on-Solway in the west to Wallsend on the River Tyne in the east. It took only 10 years to complete and was built on the orders of the Emperor Hadrian when he visited Britain in AD122. Its purpose was to keep out the "barbarians" to the north and for 300 years it was the north-west frontier of the Roman Empire which stretched east as far as present-day Iraq and south to the Sahara Desert.

1. From the opposite end of the car park to the entrance, take a surfaced path between two stone walls, through a gate, and continue on to meet Hadrian's Wall going east-west. Turn left through a gate and follow the path. When it becomes unsurfaced, follow the grassy path downhill to your right to join a stone path which drops down and then rises steeply uphill with the Wall on your right going through a squeeze stile half way up. You are now on the Hadrian's Wall Path and also the Pennine Way. Go through a gap in the stone wall at the top, through a kissing-gate and follow the footpath signs until you reach stone steps dropping down to a kissing-gate, and continue uphill. After a short stretch there is another drop to a Milecastle (Number 39) which you can enter over a stile. After another up-and-down (!) you reach Sycamore Gap where you will find the iconic isolated tree recently christened Robin Hood's Tree. It really is a dramatic sight.

Sycamore Gap is the site of the tallest piece of the surviving Wall and this wonderful sycamore tree is much photographed. Since 1991, it has been affectionately called Robin Hood's Tree, after a scene from the film *Robin*

Hood: Prince of Thieves starring Kevin Costner. In the scene, Robin meets up with the Moor, Azeem, played by Morgan Freeman, and he rescues a boy being chased by the Sheriff of Nottingham's men for killing a deer. The scene is full of poetic licence. Not only is the setting in a completely different part of the country to Nottingham but also, when Azeem wants to pray and face east, Robin points him to the south! Nevertheless, it was good to have a bit of Hollywood glamour visiting the area and it is a matter of local pride that the place was chosen. It is not the only Northumberland location to be used in the film. Maid Marion's Manor was at Hulne Priory in Alnwick and Alnwick Castle also makes an appearance.

Robin Hood's Tree

2. After the tree go through a gap in the Wall and follow the other side to reach a ladder stile, on the other side of which you start to walk along Highshield Crags high above the beautiful Crag Lough passing through a wooded area. Near the end of the Lough, cross a ladder stile into a more open area to reach a farm track crossing your path. Go right over a ladder stile back over the Wall, then cross the track, through a gate and continue along the path (signed **Housesteads 1½**). Carry on past Hotbank Farm, ignoring the footpath to the left going through the farm, and go through a kissing-gate to climb uphill along the grassy path. At the top of the rise, keep going alongside the wall and do not be tempted to take the more obvious path to the right towards a stone wall enclosing some trees. This right turn is an alternative route to Housesteads Fort along the Roman Military Way but as we are on the Wall, we shall stay on the Wall! Walk along the top of Hotbank Crags for a relieving level stretch with views of Greenlee Lough and Brownlee Lough and wind turbines far in the distance behind – a real coalescence of the old and the new. You reach another steep drop to Rapishaw Gap where we leave the Pennine Way as it goes north.

Go over a ladder stile and follow the path as it bends round to the right. Just as the ground levels out turn left uphill back to the Wall with the aid of some well-placed stones. Keep following the Wall along Cuddy's Crags and, shortly, drop down and up again passing another Milecastle (Number 37), which is very similar to the last one. Go along Housesteads Crags to reach a gate into a narrow wooded area where you are allowed to walk along the actual Wall which is just to the left of you. At the end of the wooded area you reach Housesteads Fort which is worth a visit.

There are 16 forts along Hadrian's Wall and Housesteads (*Vercovicium*) is the best preserved. It is an English Heritage site. It was occupied for about 280 years by up to 800 soldiers. The fort was built to a standard "template" which the Romans used and Housesteads is one of the best surviving examples anywhere. The largest building is the *praetorium*, the commanding officer's house, built around a courtyard. The site also contains the remains of the barrack blocks, store room, bath house, Headquarters building and even a hospital. In 2012, the museum on site re-opened after a £1 million revamp and now has some dramatic film footage and a collection of Roman artefacts including altars, tools, weapons and jewellery.

Housesteads Fort

If you do not wish to visit, then continue straight along the north side of the Fort to the eastern end and the Knag Burn Gateway where you cross the Wall through a gate. To visit the Fort, turn right through a gate in the wall just before it, and go across a field and down to the museum and ticket office. When finished, loop round the Fort towards the east to reach the Knag Burn Gateway where you stay on the same side of the Wall and turn right (signed **Sewingshields 1¾**). After a short distance, cross a step stile into a wooded area to reach a ladder stile. There is another up-and-down stretch now, but about 1km after Housesteads, you will reach a gate and a ladder stile on your left with an ornate sign on the gate saying **King's Wicket**.

On the OS map an enclosure is shown just next to King's Wicket. A wicket is a gate but the name is also applied to the earthwork enclosure, probably used for keeping animals. It is believed to be from the medieval period and associated with a drove road which passed through the wall at this point.

3. This is the start of the return leg. Cross over the King's Wicket now facing west. You will see a small plantation ahead of you to the right of the Wall. There is supposed to be a footpath to it but it is very unclear, so the best strategy is to go straight for the middle of the plantation across rough ground and using any paths that may help the journey. Cross a stile into the plantation and another one on the other side. You will see a clear path now straight ahead, and the wall to your left snaking its way westwards. Follow the path to reach a gate and a ladder stile where the Pennine Way crosses your path. Head towards some lime kilns about 350m further on. Keeping to the high ground, continue on past a plantation on your left. Crag Lough comes into view as the path gradually drops down to the left to meet a metal gate and a stile which lead to Hotbank Farm. However, you should turn right here over another stile next to a gate and head west across a field to cross a stile next to a gate into another field, on the other side of which (slightly to the right) you cross a ladder stile next to a gate. Pass a couple of barns at Long Side and walk on, taking in the view of Robin Hood's Tree this time from the north, to reach a stone wall which you cross via a ladder stile to meet another couple of barns at Peatrigg. Continue along the clear path for just over 1km

Milecastle near Crag Lough

to reach a ladder stile on to a minor road where you turn left back to the car park.

The Hadrian's Wall Path is an 84 mile route which opened in 2003 after a £6 million investment by the Countryside Agency (succeeded in 2006 by Natural England). It became the 15th National Trail in England and Wales. These National Trails resulted from similar reasons to the creation of our National Parks and Areas of Outstanding Natural Beauty – a basic desire to keep the areas "special" and protect them from development. The first national trail was, of course, the Pennine Way which opened in 1965 and crosses Hadrian's Wall on this walk.

Walk 26: Lambley Viaduct

This walk exploits some of the railway history of Northumberland, beginning near the splendid Lambley Viaduct, crossing the moors of Lambley Common and returning along a disused railway track on the South Tyne Trail.

Distance	12.8km (8.0 miles)
Difficulty	Moderate. The walk follows fairly level stretches of the Pennine Way and South Tyne Trail
Start	Grid Reference NY679595. Lambley Viaduct South Tyne Trail car park at Coanwood. To get to the start from the east, take the A69 past Hexham and on to the Haltwhistle bypass. Take the second left along the bypass on to a minor road signed Alston and Coanwood. When you reach Herdley Bank First School on your left, you are in Coanwood. A little further on, do not follow the road sign to the left signed Coanwood(!) but carry straight on for a little towards Lambley to reach the car park on your right
Parking	As above. In 2012 parking was free
Maps	OS 1:25000 Explorer OL43, Hadrian's Wall, Haltwhistle & Hexham; OS 1:50000 Landranger Sheet 86, Haltwhistle & Brampton
Refreshments	South of Coanwood is the Kirkstyle Inn which has a good reputation. It is off the A689 as you approach Slaggyford. It serves food but not every day and is not open all day. To the north, Haltwhistle has a number of places to eat and drink
Advice	This walk can be done at any time of the year but autumn is particularly good when the trees

Advice (cont'd)	along the return leg show their varied colours. The path across Lambley Common can get very boggy at times

1. Leave the car park and cross the road to a wooden gate leading on to a footpath (**Lambley Viaduct South Tyne Trail**). Just after the former Coanwood Station turn right through a large metal gate, signed **Public Right of Way Lambley Footbridge**, following the path downhill. Pass to the left of a house, and cross a stream over a footbridge into a field. Do not follow the track bending uphill, but turn right diagonally across the field towards the bottom left-hand corner and cross a stile next to a small metal gate. Follow the path along the edge of the River South Tyne and cross a footbridge just in front of the Viaduct. Go through a squeeze stile at the end of the bridge, turn left and follow the path up some steep steps to a stile. At a crossroads of paths, turn right on the footpath (**Lambley ¼**) and climb some more steps, through a gap in a wooden fence to reach a wooden gate. Ignore the footpath sign pointing through the gate and turn right just before the gate following a woodland path along the top with the river down below you on your right. Go past and round a row of houses on your left to reach a road, where you turn left and then immediately right following a footpath sign.

There was once a nunnery at Lambley just to the south of Lambley Farm which is under 1km to the north of where you have just come out. It was home to Benedictine nuns from 1132 and was founded by Adam de Tindale and his wife Heloise. In 1296 the building was destroyed in a furious and barbaric raid by the Scots under William Wallace, in which many people were killed indiscriminately, young and old. A little before this in 1279, is an amusing story about the prioress who had a disagreement with the local Baron of Thirlwell to do with grazing her cattle on his land. The Baron complained to the King's assizes and to cut a long story short, the prioress ended up challenging the Baron to single combat! However in those days, one had a champion to do one's fighting for you and when she saw that her champion was so much smaller and weaker than the Baron's she admitted defeat and coughed up the fine of £10.

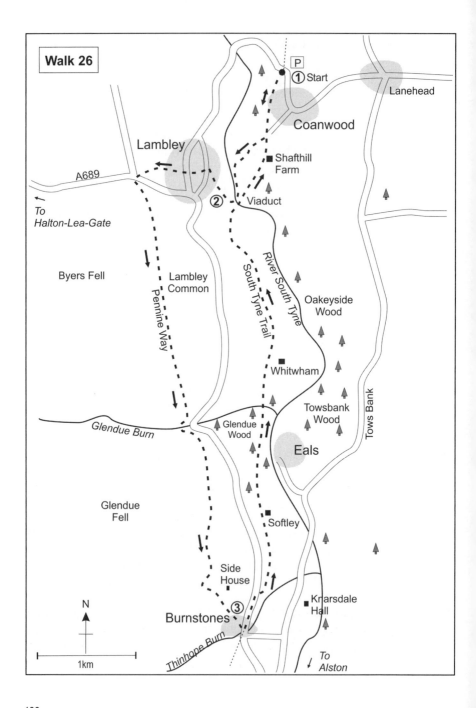

Walk 26

To Halton-Lea-Gate

Lanehead

Coanwood

P ① Start

Shafthill Farm

Lambley

A689

② Viaduct

Byers Fell

Lambley Common

Pennine Way

South Tyne Trail

River South Tyne

Oakeyside Wood

Whitwham

Glendue Burn

Glendue Wood

Towsbank Wood

Tows Bank

Eals

Glendue Fell

Softley

Side House

N

Knarsdale Hall

Burnstones ③

Thinhope Burn

To Alston

1km

2. Pass a row of cottages and walk along the path to the right of a metal gate, between some trees and a hedgerow. Go through a tunnel under a road, through a wooden gate and straight across a field passing a solitary sycamore tree to reach a kissing-gate in a stone wall. Continue straight on towards a house with a white gable end, cross a stile over a wire fence then another stile at the end of a stone wall. Continue through the grounds of the house with the house on your left and turn left in front of the house to the A689. Cross the road and through a metal gate on to a footpath (**Burnstones 3**). Follow the path uphill across Lambley Common, ignoring the path over a stile off to the right and carry straight on along what is now the Pennine Way. Follow this path for over 2km over the top of the Common going in a straight line southwards, crossing a number of stiles. As you descend towards Glendue Wood keep your eyes peeled for a wooden post just to your left. Do not go to the post but carry straight for about 100m to reach a stone step stile on your right over the wall. It is easy to miss so if you reach the wood with the wall to the right of you, you have gone too far. Cross over the wall and turn left down towards Glendue Burn where you turn left over a stile and across a footbridge. Follow the path along stone flags as it goes very close to the A698 then moves uphill away from the road to a stile in a wire fence. Cross the stile for another straight stretch of about 2km southwards to Burnstones going through a number of gates and stiles. The path is clear in some places and not so clear in others but keep straight on in a southerly direction. When you pass a stone barn and then some farm buildings on your left you should see a finger post straight ahead of you. Head towards the post (which is pointing along the Pennine Way in the direction from which you have just come) and follow the stony track downhill to the left. Go through a wooden gate in a stone wall and after about 100m at a field corner, go through a kissing-gate on your left, where the footpath has recently been legally diverted away from Knarsdale Hall which is straight ahead of you. Head right diagonally downhill across the field to a footbridge then a kissing-gate to reach a larger gate.

The buildings here are called Burnstones on the OS map and the right of way is shown going through the grounds. This path has now been diverted and the buildings seem to have been renamed Knarsdale Hall which is actually shown on the OS map to be a little to the east on the other side of

the Thinhope Burn. The Knarsdale Estate has over 10,000 acres of prime grouse-shooting moorland and was bought by the businessman Richard Kelvin-Hughes in 2007. Grouse shooting is big business, a party of nine paying upwards of £20,000 per day. There are over 135 grouse moors in England alone, many more in Scotland, and there is no shortage of takers as it is regarded as a real shooting challenge, the grouse flying like rockets, low and fast. The Knarsdale Hall on the OS map was built in the 17th century and has a ghost story attached to it. The ghost is that of the niece of the Lord of the Manor from long ago and can be seen gliding from the back door to a pond in the yard on the anniversary of her death. She had discovered that her brother, the Lord's nephew, was having an affair with the Lord's young wife. Her brother, afraid that she might inform on him, drowned her in the pond. However, one would have to keep vigil for 365 days of the year to witness this as no-one is certain of the date of her death!

3. Turn left along the A689, taking care as there is no pavement, and after about 150m turn right into a small car park and then left to join the South Tyne Trail (**Lambley Viaduct 2½**). Follow this lovely disused railway line northwards for 3.5km ignoring any paths off the main track. You will eventually reach a house with a lane crossing your path. Go straight on and a little further on, just before a gap in a wooden fence in front of you, turn right (**South Tyne trail (North), Lambley Viaduct ¼, Lambley Village ½, Haltwhistle 5**). There is a notice here saying the South Tyne Trail is incorrectly marked on the Ordnance Survey map as it shows it going straight on, rather than right. Head downhill passing the old Station House on your left, down some steps to the base of the Viaduct. Follow the path as it climbs all the way to the top of the Viaduct, passing the path crossroads which you met on the way out (this time turning left). You reach the top of the Viaduct via a metal staircase. Turn left across the Viaduct, taking in the magnificent views, and then follow the Trail for 1.2km back to the car park.

The South Tyne Trail is a 36.5km route from the source of the River South Tyne, through Alston to Haltwhistle. For much of its length it follows the route of the former Haltwhistle to Alston Branch Railway. During the Industrial Revolution, the area was mined for coal, lead and limestone and the railway was built to transport the minerals to the Newcastle to Carlisle Railway. The final link in the railway was the magnificent Lambley Viaduct

Lambley Viaduct

over the South Tyne, designed by Sir George Barclay-Bruce and opened in 1852. The railway was in use right up to 1976, acting as a vital link for the people in this remote area. The viaduct was restored in 1995-96, and opened as a footpath with glorious views over the river. The South Tyne Valley supports an unusual range of wildlife. There are rare plants which can tolerate the high level of metal toxins, for example narrow-lipped helleborine which is normally only found on chalky ground in the south of England and mountain pansy which is usually found in upland areas. The cliff or rock whitebeam is a rare tree and the valley is the only place in Northumberland where it can be found. In the river itself salmon and sea trout are present and there is a strong and increasing population of otters.

Walk 27: Allen Banks

Allen Banks is one of Northumberland's real beauty spots. This walk has been designed with three versions of different lengths, all of which incorporate a stroll along the beautiful River Allen. The longer walks also explore the stronghold of Staward Peel.

Distance	Full walk: 12.9km (8.0 miles) Medium walk: 9.6km (6.0 miles) Short walk: 4.5km (2.8 miles)
Difficulty	Short walk: easy. Medium and full walk: moderate/strenuous both involving some steep climbs
Start	Grid Reference NY798640. Allen Banks National Trust car park. To get there from the east, follow the A69 and about 5km west of Haydon Bridge, turn left at the brown National Trust sign for Allen Banks and Staward Gorge. Follow the minor road over the River South Tyne for about 1km avoiding any right turns and the car park is just past Ridley Hall on the right
Parking	As above. In 2012 parking was free for National Trust members. For non-members it was £4 for the whole day or £2 for up to 4 hours
Maps	OS 1:25000 Explorer OL43, Hadrian's Wall, Haltwhistle & Hexham; OS 1:50000 Landranger Sheet 87, Hexham & Haltwhistle
Refreshments	Bardon Mill to the west and Haydon Bridge to the east are the nearest places for food and drink
Advice	Any time of the year has its own delights in this beautiful place. However, spring is the best time to enjoy the abundance of wild flowers, and the colours in autumn are absolutely gorgeous. All the walks can be a bit muddy in places

1. Leave the car park from the opposite end to the entrance along a clear footpath following the beautiful River Allen. After a short while you reach a fork and a marker post indicating a number of trails – brown, purple and orange. Go straight on following the brown (which looks black) trail to Plankey Mill keeping next to the river. This is mixed woodland with sycamore, horse chestnut, beech and yew among others. Keep to the river ignoring any paths off to the right. Carry on past a suspension bridge and nearly 2km from the car park enter the Plankey Mill and Briarwood Banks Nature Reserve where there are some interesting information panels.

Allen Banks was donated to the National Trust in 1942 by the Honourable Francis Bowes Lyon, the brother of Queen Elizabeth II's maternal grandfather. Briarwood Banks is part the largest tract of ancient woodland in Northumberland. Many of the wonderfully evocative and mysterious names bestowed upon British wild flowers are represented here. Wood sorrel and herb Paris are indicators of ancient undisturbed woodlands, dog's mercury is often seen carpeting the floor, early purple orchids flower from April to June, enchanter's nightshade is a member of the willowherb family unrelated to deadly nightshade, and toothwort grows on the roots of woody shrubs, especially hazel. The dormouse also has its most northerly population in the woods.

2. Cross a footbridge over a burn and then a larger bridge over the River Allen to Plankey Mill. On the other side of the river turn right towards a finger post. For the medium and long walk, follow the instructions from Paragraph 3. For the short walk turn left here away from the river on a footpath (**Allen Banks car park 1¼**) through a metal gate following the brown arrow. Turn left in front of the buildings and continue uphill on the surfaced lane for 125m to a point where a path leads left down towards the river off the main track. Re-join the medium and full walks at this point and follow the instructions from Paragraph 7.

Plankey Mill is now a farm but was once a corn mill driven by a water-wheel. It is sometimes confused with Plankey Smelt Mill, on the other side of the river, the remains of which can just be made out covered with hazel. The North Pennines was a lead mining area and the ore is galena or lead sulphide. Smelting produced noxious fumes of sulphur dioxide and vapourised lead and you can see evidence of long horizontal flues leading

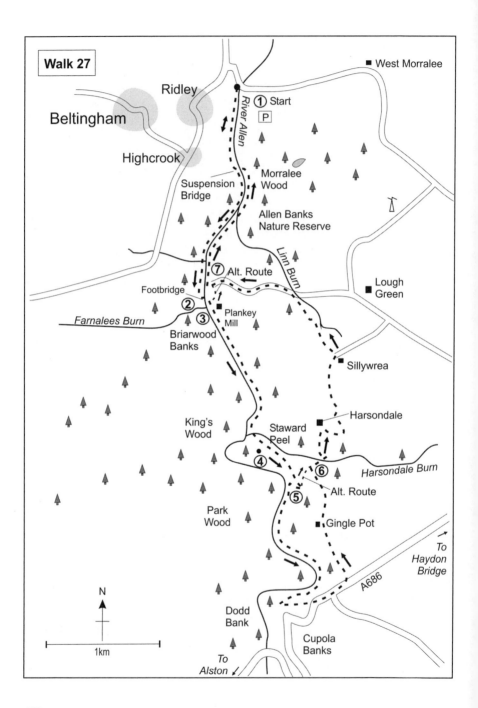

Walk 27

West Morralee

Ridley

Beltingham

Highcrook

River Allen

① Start

P

Suspension Bridge

Morralee Wood

Allen Banks Nature Reserve

Linn Burn

⑦ Alt. Route

Footbridge

Lough Green

Farnalees Burn

② ③ Plankey Mill

Briarwood Banks

Sillywrea

Harsondale

King's Wood

Staward Peel

④ ⑥

Harsondale Burn

⑤ Alt. Route

Park Wood

Gingle Pot

A686

To Haydon Bridge

N

1km

Dodd Bank

Cupola Banks

To Alston

The bridge at Plankey Mill

to tall chimneys in many parts of the North Pennines. Boys were sent into these flues to scrape condensed lead from the walls. It was a dangerous unhealthy practice.

3. Continue through a wooden gate along the footpath by the river (**Staward Pele 1, Cupolar Bridge 2½**). This is also marked as the **John Martin Heritage Trail** (burgundy arrows). Cross a field, go through a gate into another field then through a gap at the end of a wall into a third field and enter a wood through a kissing-gate. Follow the river through Scots Pine for over 600m and on the other side of a footbridge the path splits. Take the footpath left, signed **Peel**, going uphill and after a short rise, take the left prong of a fork and climb up a steep path aided by some steps. At the top you will find the remains of a farmhouse. Continue along to reach the ruins of Staward Peel where you will find some information panels.

Staward Peel (or Pele) must be one of the most impregnable sites for a fortress in Northumberland and, between 1272 and 1384, that is exactly what it was. After that it became a retreat for the brothers of Hexham Priory and this arrangement stayed until the Dissolution of the Monasteries between 1536 and 1541. During the 17th Century it fell into

ruin as the stones were used for building elsewhere. In the early 18th Century a colourful character called Dickie of Kingswood lived in the ruins. He was a thief and confidence trickster and is the subject of an amusing story. By all accounts Dickie was a non-violent man who lived by his wits and roguish charm. The story starts one night with Dickie stealing a couple of oxen from Denton Burn near Newcastle. He drove the cattle for a few days and sold them to a farmer from Lanercost who rode a fine chestnut mare which Dickie instantly coveted. That night he stole the mare and on riding back to Staward Pele encountered the farmer from Denton Burn who had been travelling on foot in search of his oxen. The farmer asked if he had seen the oxen and Dickie pointed him in the direction of Lanercost. At the same time, he sold the farmer the ill-gotten mare to aid him on his journey. Imagine the surprise when the two farmers met, each with stolen property belonging to the other!

4. Follow the path along a ridge with steep drops to the River Allen on your right and Harsondale Burn on your left. When you reach a fork, take the right path (**National Trust Path not dedicated as a public right of way**) along the top of the bank to meet a track crossing your path and a large wooden gate and stile on your left. For the full walk, follow the instructions from Paragraph 5. For the medium walk, turn left over the stile and head across a field to the left of a grassy mound. There is no clear path but head towards the wood to a stile where a stone wall meets a wire fence along the edge of the wood. Re-join the long walk at this point and follow the instructions from Paragraph 6.

John Martin (1789-1854) after whom the Heritage Trail is named, was born in Haydon Bridge and was one of the most popular painters of his day. The trail was opened in 2006 to commemorate the 150th anniversary of his death as the area had a heavy influence on his paintings. He specialised in large canvases of the ancient world in chaos, exemplified by *Belshazzar's Feast* which when it was exhibited in 1821 had to be cordoned off to keep the crowds at bay. After being overlooked for many years, he is now again highly regarded. He is sometimes referred to as "Mad Martin" but this name applies more to his brother Jonathan who set fire to York Minster and was placed in the lunatic asylum of Bedlam as a result. His two other brothers were colourful eccentrics. One of them, William, used to walk along Newcastle Quayside wearing a tortoise shell for a hat! Ever an energetic and curious man, John Martin had many other interests, at one

time attempting to solve London's sewage problems, the designs for which turned out to be very good and influential.

5. At the wooden gate and stile, turn right downhill and after about 200m, turn left at a fork along a narrow path, taking care as there is a very steep drop to the right, and continue down to the riverbank. Follow the river for a glorious riverside stroll through mixed woodland eventually rising steeply above it. The Ordnance Survey map shows a short footpath going off to the left as you climb this bank, but it does not appear to be there on the ground. When you reach a split in the path at the top of the bank, take the more obvious path to the left to a stile over a wire fence and a footpath sign pointing left which you take. Go along the field edge and cross a ladder stile over a stone wall on to the A686. Turn left carefully along the busy road, going straight on past the junction to Allendale and Catton, and about 100m further on take the footpath left (**Gingle Pot ½**) across a field. Cross a ladder stile into another field

The River Allen

and follow the path to the ruin at Gingle Pot to another ladder stile. Go alongside a stone wall (wall on your right) and continue on when the wall ends to meet a stile in a wire fence along the edge of a wood. This is where the medium walk re-joins the full walk.

The historian William Weaver Tomlinson, author of the amazingly detailed *Comprehensive Guide to Northumberland*, stopped at Gingle Pot on one of his walks in 1888 to boil water for tea. The remains of the fireplace, flue and boiler probably used by Tomlinson can still be found in the undergrowth. There used to be a station at nearby Staward on the Hexham to Allendale Railway (the building at Staward Halt is now a private house) and a popular day out was to travel to the station and walk to Staward Gorge past Gingle Pot.

6. Cross over the stile into the wood following the path downhill and across a footbridge over the Harsondale Burn. Climb very steeply uphill to a stile into a field and head towards the right-hand corner of a line of bushes. Then follow the field boundary to Harsondale Farm where you cross a ladder stile and turn right along the farm track. As the track sweeps left go through a metal gate or over a stile to your left into a field and continue alongside the stone wall on your left. Cross a stone step stile and then immediately turn right along a stone wall to a wooden stile where you turn sharp left along the field edge. Walk downhill along the field boundary, crossing a couple of stiles until you reach Sillywrea Farm. At the farm go between a wooden barn and a stone building over a stile and turn right along a track. Just in front of the farm buildings turn left through a double metal gate along a stony track between two stone walls (in 2012, there was no footpath sign here). Where the left wall ends go through a metal gate and follow the path as it bends right along the right wall which becomes a barbed-wire fence. Cross a stile next to a red metal gate and continue alongside the Linn Burn to cross another stile next to a gate by a rather grand oak tree. Follow the field edge to a kissing-gate and come out on a narrow road where you turn left. Go downhill towards Plankey Mill and after just over 600m you meet the brown trail turning right downhill almost back on yourself. This is where we re-join the short walk.

Sillywrea Farm has been the subject of a Tyne-Tees television programme and also a book: *The Last Horsemen* written by Charles Bowden and

published in 2011. The farm is the last in Britain to be powered solely by horses, which work the land and do all the ploughing. As you walk across the fields, you may well see one or more of these large Clydesdale horses. The farmer John Dodd has passed on his passion for horses to his son-in-law and grandson. Sillywrea is also known as "quiet corner" and let us hope that this traditional peaceful way of life will continue for years to come.

7. Follow the path downhill past a small ruin, through a kissing-gate and descend very close to the river. Continue along the brown trail for about 1.2km passing through a deep gorge to reach a split in the path where the brown trail goes left downhill and the purple trail continues straight on. Follow the brown trail as it zig-zags down to the suspension bridge. Cross the bridge and turn right along the path back to the car park.

Clydesdale horse at Sillywrea Farm

Walk 28: Corbridge – South

This walk together with Walk 29 makes a figure of eight walk, with Corbridge in the middle. They can be done separately or in one go. The two together would make an excellent weekend break as Corbridge is a lovely place to stay. This south loop goes through the pleasant woods, fields and country lanes to the south of Corbridge returning along the River Tyne.

Distance	8.1km (5.0 miles)
Difficulty	Moderate. There are a few climbs but nothing too taxing
Start	Grid Reference NY988640. Car park off the roundabout at the south end of the bridge over the river at Corbridge
Parking	In 2012, parking was free
Maps	OS 1:25000 Explorer OL43, Hadrian's Wall, Haltwhistle & Hexham; OS 1:50000 Landranger Sheet 87, Hexham & Haltwhistle
Refreshments	There are plenty of places to eat and drink in Corbridge
Advice	The car park can get full especially in the summer months as Corbridge is quite a tourist attraction. So get there early. Corbridge is also a stop on the Newcastle to Carlisle railway, so this is an option if you don't want to bring the car. Parts of the walk can get muddy so come prepared

1. From the car park, cross to the other side of the roundabout on to the right hand pavement of the B6529 which is actually signed for Prudhoe and Gateshead (A695). Head in a southerly direction away from Corbridge, past Corbridge station and over the railway. As the road bends to the left, there are a couple of road mirrors for drivers to see round the bend, and just after that there are some steps leading up to the right which you should take. They can be hidden by undergrowth and there is no footpath sign, so keep your eyes

peeled. The steps lead on to a path through a wood and at the right time of year you can smell the wild garlic. Go through a kissing-gate at the end of a wood into a field, where you turn left following the edge of the field, cross a stile over a wooden fence and then cross the A695 and over another wooden stile (footpath sign **Mountpleasant** ¼). Follow the edge of a field to reach a wooden stile into Ladycutters Lane, where you turn right ignoring the footpath straight ahead.

At Corbridge Station is the Valley Restaurant, one of the best Indian restaurants in the country. In 2012 it came fourth in the Tiffin Cup, an annual competition held at the House of Commons to find the best South Asian restaurant in the United Kingdom. The restaurant is famous for its Passage to India Train Service, locally known as the Curry Train. Customers can book return travel to Newcastle Central station and a four-course dinner and, during the journey, place orders and receive service from restaurant staff. It's a novel experience.

2. Follow the surfaced lane until it reaches a house called West Fell and carry straight on along the unsurfaced path between a hedge and a wall. Go through a wooden gate into a grassy area with some bushes and follow the hedge. The area soon becomes a large open field. Continue through a wooden gate and carry straight on to reach a fork soon after. Take the left hand path up through the woods. Follow this path along the edge of the wood with fields on your right ignoring any paths off to the left. After about 600m the path enters an area with trees on both sides and you should keep climbing on the main track ignoring paths leading off downhill. You will reach a gate with a field on the other side. Do not go through this but turn left still going uphill. When you come out of the woods turn right through a gate (footpath sign) and continue through a field with a stone wall on your left. You eventually reach the top of your climb and go through two metal gates into another field at the end of which is a wooden gate on to a minor road. Turn left and go gently uphill past Temperley Grange. At a junction, carry straight on (signed **Prospect Hill** ½) to reach a crossroads where you turn left (signed **Corbridge** 1½). Follow the road past a farm where it bends sharp left and then curves round to the right steadily going downhill. When you reach another sharp bend to the left, turn right on to a drive and immediately left over a stone stile on to a footpath signed **Ravenstone** ¼. Go straight across a field, past a large ash tree

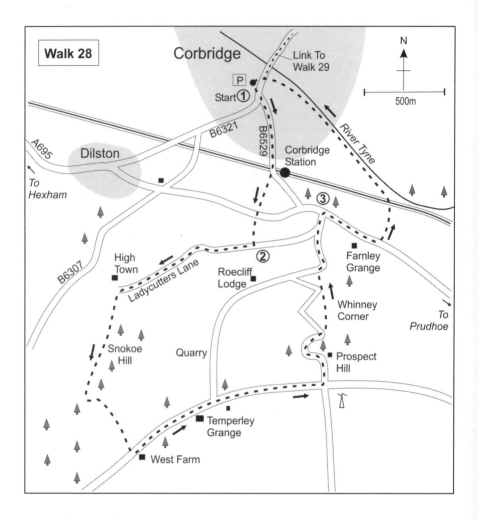

and cross a ladder stile at the bottom of the field into another field. Turn half left and head downhill aiming just to the left of a very large ash tree to reach a step stile over a stone wall on to the road. Turn right and follow the road to the A695.

The original plan for this walk was to follow the River Tyne west from the car park, and then follow the Devil's Water south to Dilston Castle. However, this plan was thwarted when The North Pennines Heritage Trust, who managed the Dilston Castle site, went into administration, and as a result the whole

site was closed to the public. Hopefully it will open again in the future, but the stories relating to it are so atmospheric that they are worth recounting. First of all, Devil's Water, which flows close to the castle, has nothing to do with the devil at all. It is named after the Dyvelstons whose original name was D'Eivill, a family who built a castle on the site in the 14th Century. The most famous name associated with the castle is the ill-fated James, Earl of Derwentwater, who was executed on Tower Hill in 1716 for his part in the failed Jacobite rebellion of 1715. On the night of his execution, 24th February 1716, an unusually bright display of the Aurora Borealis occurred (other accounts say it was a meteor) which turned the Devil's Water blood red and the skies a glowing crimson. This phenomenon was known as Lord Derwentwater's Lights for many years afterwards. Before he took part in the rebellion, James had been hiding from government agents in a number of places in Northumberland, one of which is said to be the cave beneath the Devil's Punchbowl, a rock on Shaftoe Crags, near Bolam Lake. So, the Devil seems to have an ominous presence in Northumberland! The Devil's Causeway (a Roman road) and the Devil's Lapful near Kielder are further examples.

3. Cross the A695 and turn right along the pavement. Just after East Lodge Farnley at a bus stop, turn left through a wooden gate on to a footpath (**Corbridge 1¼**). Go along the edge of a field with a hedge on your left. It leads to a stile which you cross and head down some steps turning right at the bottom. Cross a railway line (taking care as this is a main line) to the banks of the River Tyne and turn left along a pleasant riverside path. Go past Tynedale Park sports ground to reach Corbridge Cricket Club where you can either follow the unsurfaced road back to the car park or, for a more pleasant stroll, enter a wooded area on your right and follow paths closer to the river which also lead back to the car park.

There has been a bridge over the River Tyne in Corbridge since 1235, although there is evidence of a Roman Bridge a little further along the river. The original medieval bridge, the remains of which can be seen at low water, became badly damaged and hazardous in the 17th Century because of frequent flooding. The present bridge was erected in 1674 and is extremely strong with seven wide arches. It is the only bridge on the whole of the River Tyne to remain standing after the severe flooding of 1771. The water was so high that people were said to have leaned over the bridge parapet to wash their hands.

Walk 29: Corbridge – North

This walk together with Walk 28 makes a figure of eight walk, with Corbridge in the middle. They can be done separately or in one go. The two together would make an excellent weekend break as Corbridge is a lovely place to stay. This north loop goes through Corbridge to the exquisite Aydon Castle and returns to Corbridge for a more detailed exploration of this historic town.

Distance	8.8km (5.5 miles)
Difficulty	Moderate. There are a few climbs but nothing too taxing
Start	Grid Reference NY988640. Car park off the roundabout at the south end of the bridge over the river at Corbridge
Parking	In 2012, parking was free
Maps	OS 1:25000 Explorer 316, Newcastle-upon-Tyne and Explorer OL43, Hadrian's Wall, Haltwhistle & Hexham; OS 1:50000 Landranger Sheet 87, Hexham & Haltwhistle
Refreshments	There are plenty of places to eat and drink in Corbridge
Advice	The car park can get full especially in the summer months as Corbridge is quite a tourist attraction. So get there early. Corbridge is also a stop on the Newcastle to Carlisle railway, so this is an option if you don't want to bring the car. There are so many historic sites and buildings in and near Corbridge, that it is worth taking your time on this walk, even a whole day. Aydon Castle and Corbridge Roman Town are both English Heritage sites and are open to the public. As they are not open every day or all year round, you should check them out beforehand

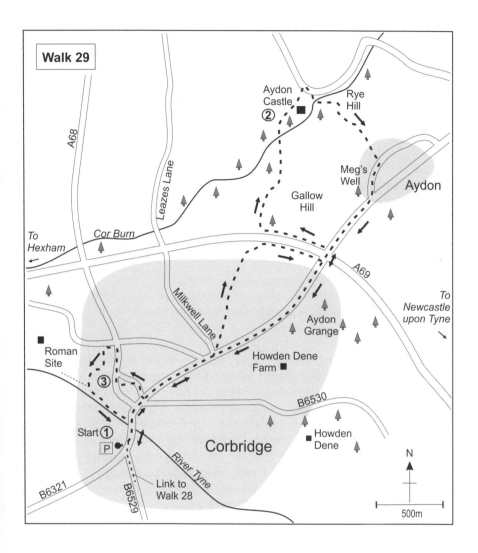

1. From the car park, turn left over the bridge into Corbridge. At the crossroads, go straight across towards the Golden Lion and follow the road straight on (Princes Street) to the right of the pub. This is the B6321 and you follow this as it rises gently out of town. Just after Corbridge First School, turn left on to Milkwell Lane and then immediately right on to Deadridge Lane (bridleway sign **Aydon Road ½**, **Aydon Castle 1½**). Keep straight on as the metalled lane

gives way to a grassy track to reach the A69 where you turn right in an easterly direction following the south side of the road. After about 400m go through a gate on to the B6321 and turn left over the A69, then immediately turn left through a gate on to a bridleway (**Aydon Castle 1¼**). Follow this for another 400m west parallel to the north side of the A69. When you reach a stone wall in front of you, turn sharp right and follow the wall to reach a wooden gate. Enter a field through the gate and go straight on with a stone wall now on your right. The wall gives way to a wire fence and you should go through a gate in this fence to your right. Follow the path initially straight on and then sweeping round to the left across the field to reach a gate into a wood. Go through the wood, taking in the smell of wild garlic, and the path eventually drops down to an idyllic spot by a footbridge over the Cor Burn which makes a nice place for a picnic. Cross the footbridge and follow the path uphill. As you rise, Aydon Castle comes into view and you should head to the top to a wooden gate in a stone wall, cross a short field, then through another wooden gate to come out at the entrance to Aydon Castle

Aydon Castle is an English Heritage site and is one of the finest examples of a 13th Century English manor house in the country. It is in a beautiful position above the wooded slopes of the Cor Burn. The walls are very thick and it was regarded as a place of great strength. It has passed through the hands of several families and during the 14th Century was attacked by the Scots a number of times. Below the Castle is a rock called Jack's Leap which got its name from a Scottish trooper who escaped when the rest of his party were being thrown off the cliff. The Castle is unoccupied but much of it is intact and enclosed. There are interesting information panels throughout the house and it is well worth a visit.

2. After visiting the castle, turn right at the entrance and follow the road to reach a junction where you go over a stone step stile in a wall on your right on to a footpath (**Aydon ½**) leading down some steps to the Cor Burn. Cross a footbridge and follow the path which sweeps quite steeply up to the left to reach a stile at the top of the bank. Go straight on across the field to its highest point where Aydon Village will come into sight. Head for Aydon and at a stone gatepost follow a tractor track through a metal gate on to a minor road. Turn right and follow the road to meet the B6321 where you

Aydon Castle

turn right again and make your way back over the A69, keeping to the road until you reach the Golden Lion (about 2¼km). Take care as some of the road does not have a pavement, so you have to walk on the verge. At the Golden Lion, cross the road and turn right into Hill Street. Just before the church, turn left into a narrow street past the Vicar's Pele and turn right at the market place. Go round St Andrew's Church on to Watling Street, taking in the King's Oven and head towards the Wheatsheaf Hotel.

There is so much of interest in Corbridge that it is difficult to know where to start. It was the site of an important Roman station and has had a turbulent past having been burnt by the Scots three times in the 13th and 14th Centuries. Spend some time exploring the area round the market-place. St Andrew's Church is of interest as it is one of the few churches in Northumberland which still has some Anglo-Saxon remains. It also has a large collection of stained glass windows all made between 1864 and 1975. The Vicar's Pele is a fortified tower built around AD 1300 using Roman stones from

the Hadrian's Wall area. The King's Oven is in the wall of the churchyard and was used as a communal oven until the 19th Century. The Old Market Cross had stood for 600 years until it was removed in 1807. It was restored and re-erected in 1975. Corbridge also has a good selection of specialist shops (including some fine antique shops) and there are a number of tearooms, restaurants and pubs.

The King's Oven

3. Follow the main road round the Wheatsheaf (now Stagshaw Road) ignoring the bridleway to West Green on the bend near the pub. When you reach Trinity Terrace turn left and then, after 100 metres, left again on to a footpath (**West Green ¼**). If you continue straight on along the road instead of turning left to West Green, after just over 500m, you will reach the Corbridge Roman Town site. You could visit this and then return to the footpath, or wait till later and drive there. Follow the footpath past Town Barns (where Catherine Cookson lived for a while) to reach a lane where you turn

The old market cross in Corbridge

right on to a cobbled path past a Georgian house called Orchard Vale and then left to reach a lane crossing your path. Cross a green slightly to your left to the river and then turn left along the riverside path back to the bridge. Climb up to the bridge and back to the car park.

The Corbridge Roman Town is an English Heritage site and is a little gem of a place to visit. Not as famous as the Hadrian's Wall sites of Vindolanda or Housesteads it is often overlooked by visitors to the area. It is a site which was occupied for longer than any other along Hadrian's Wall. It is at the intersection of Dere Street (going north/south) and Stanegate (going east/west) and is the only place in Britain where you can walk along the original surface of a Roman high street. It has a fascinating museum, one of the highlights of which is the contents of the Corbridge Hoard. This is the remains of a wooden chest, only discovered in 1964, which contained a mix of tools, weapons, personal items and pieces of Roman segmented armour. It was this last discovery which enabled specialists to understand in detail how this armour fitted together. The museum has an excellent interactive display about the Hoard. There are many other interesting artefacts in the museum including the famous Corbridge Lion and the Corbridge Lanx.

Corbridge Roman Town

Walk 30: Blanchland

This walk takes you up on the moors from the beautiful unspoilt village of Blanchland. It passes some of the region's lead mining heritage and the return leg following the Beldon Burn and then the River Derwent is really special.

Distance	15.5km (9.6 miles)
Difficulty	Moderate/Strenuous. There are no really steep ascents but some of the ground is rough
Start	Grid Reference NY965504. Blanchland car park just north (about 100m) of the main village
Parking	As above. In 2012, parking was free but there is an honesty box with a suggested £1 donation
Maps	The walk straddles OS 1:25000 Explorer OL43, Hadrians' Wall, Haltwhistle & Hexham and Explorer 307, Consett & Derwent Reservoir; OS 1:50000 Landranger Sheet 87, Hexham & Haltwhistle
Refreshments	The excellent White Monk Tea Room is open every day between 10.30 and 5.00. The Lord Crewe Arms is a very historic and wonderful hotel. It was closed in 2012 for refurbishment and is expected to be open again in March 2013
Advice	It can get pretty bleak on the moors in bad weather so come prepared with map, compass and suitable clothing. Beware of adders which are present on the open moorland

The village of Blanchland lies in the very south of Northumberland, in the North Pennines, an Area of Outstanding Natural Beauty second only in size to the Cotswolds. It certainly is one of the loveliest villages in Northumberland being hidden away in a deep hollow among the surrounding heather moors. It is such a picturesque and unspoilt setting that it has been used as a film location in a number of films including

The gatehouse at Blanchland

Michael Winterbottom's 1996 film of Thomas Hardy's Jude the Obscure starring Kate Winslett and Christopher Eccleston. A number of Catherine Cookson's TV films such as *The Gambling Man* and *A Dinner of Herbs* also used the village as a location.

The village gets its name from the white habits of the monks of the Premonstratensian Order which was founded on Christmas night in 1121 by St Norbert in Laon, North-East France. The monks were based in Blanchland Abbey built in 1165 by Walter de Bolbec in memory of his father. The Abbey was closed by Henry VIII in 1539 as part of the Dissolution of the Monasteries. In 1709 it was bought by Lord Crewe, the Bishop of Durham, who, on his death in 1721, left the village and estate to the Lord Crewe Charitable Trust which still owns it today. Although the Abbey no longer exists, it has noticeably shaped the village. The Abbott's House and quarters are now part of the Lord Crewe Arms Hotel. The church of St Mary the Virgin is a portion of the ruins of the Abbey Church and has some very interesting display panels about the history of Blanchland. The Post Office is housed in the ancient gatehouse next to the archway and still has a white Victorian post box, one of only three in the country, which survived an attempt to paint it red, when the then postmistress, Hilda Askew, put her foot down!

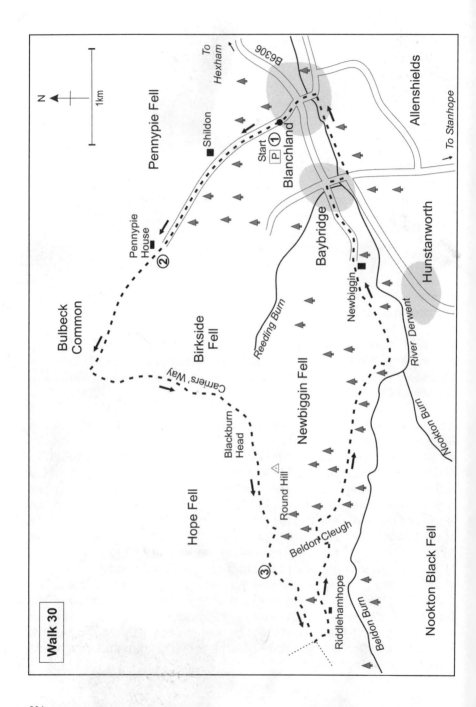

Walk 30

To Hexham

To Stanhope

B6306

Allenshields

Pennypie Fell

Shildon

Start
P ①

Blanchland

Hunstanworth

Pennypie House ②

Baybridge

Newbiggin

River Derwent

Bulbeck Common

Birkside Fell

Reeding Burn

Nookton Burn

Carrier's Way

Blackburn Head

Hope Fell

Round Hill

Newbiggin Fell

Beldon Cleugh

③

Nookton Black Fell

Riddlehamhope

Beldon Burn

N

1km

1. From the entrance to the car park, turn left up a lane alongside the Shildon Burn, ignoring a bridleway (**Coat House** or **Cote House**) and then a footpath (**Baybridge**) to your left. Then ignore two footpaths close together on your right (**Blanchland** and **Blanchland Moor**) and continue straight uphill passing the ruined buildings of the Shildon lead mine on your left. 2km from the car park at the top of the rise you reach a farm with the intriguing name of Pennypie House.

In the 19th Century, lead mining was a massive industry in the North Pennines. Evidence of it is all over the area, and the region is home to the award winning North of England Lead Mining Museum at Killhope near Allenheads which is a fully restored 19th Century lead mine with a working waterwheel (the Killhope Wheel). The Shildon lead mine, passed along the way, is reminiscent of the ones found in Cornwall as the engine-house is of a similar build.

Pennypie House is on an old drove road and was used as a place to stop for refreshments. It sold pies for a penny each, hence its name.

The engine house at Shildon

2. Do not follow the track round to the right but go straight ahead through a wooden five-bar gate. Keep straight on along a path (**Ladycross, Burntshield Haugh**) alongside a stone wall until you reach a bend to the right after about 100m where you leave the track and go straight on along a footpath (**Burntshield Haugh 1¾**) over the moor. After about 500m and a couple of marker posts you reach a ladder stile over a stone wall. Cross the stile and go half left following the marker posts for almost 1km rising and then descending to a bridleway crossing your path. This is the Carriers' Way, an ancient packhorse route, and you should turn left here. Follow the clear path southwards for about 1.8km through a number of gates, ignoring paths off to the left and right until you get to a stone hut which you pass on your left (it is usually open if you need a rest and some shelter). You soon reach a wide moorland path on which you turn right and after a very short distance (less than 100m) leave this path half left on to a less obvious path (**do not take the more obvious path to the right which goes way off track**). The path becomes less and less distinct but keep straight on going ever so slightly downhill following the contour of the hill. You will reach a wood on the edge of a wide valley (**Beldon Cleugh**) crossing your path. At the edge of the wood turn right following the barbed wire fence with a stone wall behind it going downhill along rough ground. When you get to the edge of the wood you will see the wide valley down to your left. Continue straight on along the shelf of the valley to reach a narrow path which gradually descends to the valley floor.

Beldon Cleugh is an unusually shaped, flat-bottomed, glacial overflow channel. Many natural features in the Northumberland landscape have Scottish names. "Cleugh" is a Scottish word for ravine or valley and the similar word "heugh" is a crag or steep-sided valley. "Haugh" is an area of flat land by a river and the word "law" is often used in the names of hills e.g. Cushat Law, Yarnspath Law and Hazely Law in the Cheviot Hills.

3. The path becomes clearer and clearer and reaches a stile on a wooden planked path which you cross to the other side of the valley to a large sheepfold on your left. Follow the path uphill and carry straight on at the top across a moor keeping parallel to some woods on your left to reach a stile over a barbed-wire fence which you cross and turn left along a stony track. Do not follow the track

right to Heatheryburn but carry straight on to a wooden gate. On the other side of the gate follow a grassy path alongside a stone wall as it sweeps downhill to the left to reach the abandoned and ruined farm at Riddlehamhope. The building is in a dangerous state of disrepair so do not be tempted to go inside. From Riddlehamhope follow the clear path eastwards for over 4.5km on a delightful walk across moorland, plantations of Scots pine and fields passing through gates and over ladder stiles to reach Newbiggin Farm where the track becomes surfaced. If you are lucky you may spot a red squirrel in the wooded areas. Follow the road downhill to the pretty village of Baybridge. At a road junction, turn right and enter County Durham, pass the Baybridge picnic area and across the bridge over the River Derwent, which forms about 1½km upstream at Gibraltar Rock, where the Nookton and Beldon Burns meet. On the other side of the bridge, just after the road junction, take the footpath left for a lovely stretch which leads high above the river through woodland to reach the road where you turn left back into Blanchland.

Riddlehamhope

Riddlehamhope was abandoned in the 1970s. There are very few records about it. It is now a ruin, but was at one time a rather grand Victorian hunting lodge. It was reportedly visited by the Duchess of Connaught (1860 – 1917) and a man named Robert Lowdon appears as a gamekeeper at Riddlehamhope in the 1911 census. There are outbuildings just to the west of it and just to the west of these are the ruins of an older building, believed to be the remains of a bastle house from the 16th or 17th centuries.

Bibliography

Baker, Edward, *Walking the Cheviots*, Sigma Leisure, 1996.

Beckensall, Stan, *Northumberland's Hidden History*, Amberley Publishing, 2009

Blight, Graham (Editor), *The North East and Yorkshire – Exploring Woodland*, Frances Lincoln, 2008

Breeze, David, *Hadrian's Wall* revised reprint, English Heritage, 2011

Bulmer, Jane et al., *The Grace Darling Museum*, Jarrold Publishing 2009 and available from the museum

Dixon, David Dippie, *Upper Coquetdale, Northumberland*, Robert Redpath, first published in 1903

Duerden, Frank, B*est walks in Northumberland* revised edition, Frances Lincoln 2007

Emmett, Charlie (Compiler), *100 Walks in Northumberland*, Crowood Press, first published 1992

Gillham, John et al., *50 Walks in Durham and Northumberland*, AA Publishing, 2003

Green, Martin, *The Delavals – a Family History*, Powdene Publicity, 2007

Hall, Alan, *Walking in Northumberland*, Cicerone Press, 1998

Hallewell, Richard, *Walk Northumbria*, Bartholomew, 1990

Mee, Arthur (Editor), *The King's England – Northumberland*, Hodder and Stoughton, first published in 1952.

Morgan, Joan, *Tales of Old Northumberland*, Countryside Books, 2006

Reid, Mark, *The Inn Way to Northumberland*, Inn Way Publications, 2004

Sterry, Paul,*The Collins Complete Guide to British Wild Flowers*, HarperCollins, 2006

Sterry, Paul,*The Collins Complete Guide to British Trees*, HarperCollins, 2007

Sterry, Paul,*The Collins Complete Guide to British Birds*, HarperCollins, 2004

Tomlinson, William Weaver, *Comprehensive Guide to the County of Northumberland* 11th Edition, William H. Robinson, first published 1888

Watson, Keith, *North Country Walks 3*, The Northern Echo, 1991

Woodhouse, Robert, *Northumberland – Strange but True*, the History Press, 2008